The Glory of Man

The Glory of Man

David E. Jenkins

SCM PRESS LTD

334 00542 6

First published 1967
by SCM Press Ltd
26–30 Tottenham Road London N1 4BZ
Third impression 1984

Printed in Great Britain by
Richard Clay (The Chaucer Press) Ltd
Bungay, Suffolk

CONTENTS

PREFACE

THE PURPOSE of the lectures which follow, and which are set out more or less as I delivered them, is to raise a question of truth and to investigate a matter of faith. I wished to put to the test my growing conviction that the two questions 'What is really involved in being a man?' and 'What is truly involved in believing in Jesus Christ?' are inextricably bound up with one another and that both need a great deal of re-thinking.

I have attempted, therefore, to produce a set of lectures which theologically speaking discuss christology, and generally speaking discuss man.

The grounds for continuing to insist in the second half of the twentieth century that humanism inevitably involves theology must be gathered from the lectures themselves. They are designed and intended as an exercise in experimental thinking provoked by data for the status of which I argue as I go along. I do not expect to establish truth. I attempt to report what I believe I have seen, to sketch out what I hope to see, and perhaps to contribute something of weight to be used in the search which we must each one of us make for ourselves.

Both Christians and non-Christians need, I think, to be required pretty sharply to re-consider what they are really talking about in the current debates about God, Jesus, man and the world. The best thing about these debates is that they have ceased to be a matter for experts alone, but they are clearly too serious to be pursued with a sort of slovenly eclecticism. Each man must have broader reasons than his own choice for choosing to enter the debate at the point he does or for pursuing it in the manner he does. Hence I have felt obliged to range as widely as I could and as competently as I could without obscuring the shape of my argument and my search in the sort of details appropriate to technical discussions between experts in limited fields. And I think it would have hindered rather than helped the purpose with which the lectures were composed had I written them up for publication in a much longer form in which I attempted to bolster their arguments with as much detail as possible. I wish to argue with and on behalf of thinking men in general rather than to pursue scholarly debates.

None the less it would be entirely foreign to the spirit of open and rigorous research which I believe to be demanded in investigating both questions of truth and matters of faith, if I attempted to shelter from detailed criticism by taking refuge in broad arguments. I can scarcely hope that my competence has adequately extended even as far as I have attempted to range in these lectures, and there is clearly need to range much more widely. But what I have said, I have said in the belief that my statement will stand detailed investigation over a wide enough range and at sufficient depth to sustain enough of the argument. While, therefore, I do not address myself to experts, I have no right and no wish to avoid them.

I have added a postscript to the lectures for the reasons stated in it. I am unable to conceive of any present theological or philosophical undertaking as being an end in itself. If it has any validity it must be as a contribution to a continuing enterprise and enquiry. Hence I could not avoid ending the spoken lectures with a question mark and the published version with a postscript designed as a preface to something further. I hope that the lectures sufficiently reflect my conviction that neither in theory nor in practice should there be any conflict between absolute commitment to Jesus Christ and complete openness to the future.

our Lord and Saviour Jesus Christ—upon the Divinity of the Holy Ghost—upon the Articles of the Christian Faith, as comprehended in the Apostles' and Nicene Creeds.

'Also I direct, that thirty copies of the eight Divinity Lecture Sermons shall be always printed, within two months after they are preached; and one copy shall be given to the Chancellor of the University, and one copy to the Head of every College, and one copy to the Mayor of the city of Oxford, and one copy to be put into the Bodleian Library; and the expense of printing them shall be paid out of the revenue of the Land or Estates given for establishing the Divinity Lecture Sermons; and the Preacher shall not be paid nor be entitled to the revenue, before they are printed.

'Also I direct and appoint, that no person shall be qualified to preach the Divinity Lecture Sermons, unless he has taken the degree of Master of Arts at least, in one of the two Universities of Oxford or Cambridge; and that the same person shall never preach the Divinity Lecture Sermons twice.'

I

Our Concern

THE BAMPTON LECTURES of 1866 were delivered by the Reverend Henry Parry Liddon, student of Christ Church. They were entitled *The Divinity of Our Lord and Saviour Jesus Christ*. In his summing up towards the end of his eighth lecture, Liddon said: 'The doctrine of Christ's Divinity does not merely bind us to the historic past, and above all to the first records of Christianity; it is at this hour the strength of the Christian Church. There are forces abroad in the world of thought which, if viewed by themselves, might well make a Christian fear for the future of Christendom and of humanity. It is not merely that the Church is threatened with the loss of possessions secured to her by the reverence of centuries, and of a place of honour which has perhaps guarded civilization more effectively than it has strengthened religion. The Church has once triumphed without these gifts of Providence, and, if God wills, she can again dispense with them. But never since the first years of the Gospel was fundamental Christian truth denied and denounced so largely with such passionate animosity, as is the case at this moment in each of the most civilized nations of Europe.' (pp. 746f.)

Now, after one hundred further years of the Debate about God and Christianity, passionate animosity to fundamental Christian truth is not our immediate and obvious problem. Rather we would seem to be faced with a good deal of uncertainty as to what fundamental Christian truth is. In particular, not all Christians would themselves seem to be prepared to agree with Liddon that, 'The doctrine of Christ's Divinity . . . is at this hour the strength of the Christian Church.' Perhaps, therefore, we should proceed to inquire what is at this hour the strength of the Christian Church. But we cannot really start here, for the real question pressed upon us at and by the present time is not 'What is the strength of the Christian Church?' at all. The real, pressing and timely question is 'Why give any time or thought to enquiring into what is or was or might be the strength of the Christian Church?'

In 1866 Liddon saw the Church threatened with loss of possessions, reverence and a place of honour, although he did not see this threat as necessarily hurtful—indeed, he hints that it might well be liberating. Today, one hundred years later, the Church of England has certainly still not lost all possessions and still retains at least formally not a few places of honour. In the University of Oxford, for example, the statutes continue to require regular University sermons marked as formal and honourable acts of the University by the presence of the Vice Chancellor and Proctors. But all this sort of thing presents the appearance much more of a survival of something that was honourable and powerful in the past rather than the presence of something that is generally relevant now and vital for the future. It would be unrealistic as things are today to start an investigation into what may be held to be the fundamental truth of Christianity and into what may be claimed as the real strength of the Christian Church with the unexamined presupposition that such an enquiry is, of course, worthwhile. We must rather ask why we should now be concerned with an investigation into the truths asserted as part of Christianity, the doctrines put forward by the Christian Church, the claims of divinity for Jesus Christ, or, indeed, with any of the things concerning Jesus. What grounds are there for claiming that such concerns should be the concern of men and women in general?

I assume one ground which I take to be self-evident, universal and inescapable. I assume that our concern is with persons. If it is not, then I assert that our concern *ought* to be with persons. To refuse or ignore this concern is a failure to face up to what is involved in being a human being. To reject a concern with persons which is commensurate with the concern which persons as such demand is a refusal to face facts which amounts to a fundamental error of judgement about value. It is also a rejection of value, an attitude of immorality, which flies in the face of recognizable facts. People who refuse a proper concern for persons are immoral as human beings and wrong as judges of matters of fact.

If a man refuses to be concerned with persons in a manner which seeks to respond properly to the fact that they are persons, then he is refusing to face up to reality. By this I mean that he is failing to take account both of what is really the case and of what really matters in the case as it is. It is for this reason that I assert that our concern ought to be with persons. This assertion is not merely commending a possible attitude or describing an optional concern. It is saying that whatever concerns people may in fact show themselves to have by the ways in which they occupy their lives, none the less every human being is under a compulsion, *both factual and moral*, to be concerned with persons.

At least two apparently rash and currently unfashionable claims are contained in or implied by such a statement of concern. The first is that it is possible with reason and persuasiveness to demand general assent to a universal truth of some significance about human beings as such. The most prevalent current presupposition would seem to be that it is possible at most to make limited generalizations about recognizably limited groups of human beings from limited stand-points, such as those of biology or sociology or psychology. And that when we get on to claims about values no universal statements are permissible at all. The second difficult claim is that values are inherently present in facts or that there are some matters of fact (in this case—what is in fact involved in being a person) which demand a certain evaluation because of their inherent observable nature. Difficult and awkward as these claims are, I make them deliberately and unhesitatingly, for they seem to me to be plainly involved in this concern with persons and for persons which I find as an inescapable and demanding feature of my living and which I put forward as an inescapable demand on the living of every man and woman.

But what is this inherent observable nature of what is in fact involved in being a person, which calls for the sort of claim I am attempting to establish? You must look and see. You must consider in what ways it matters to you to be you, keeping your investigation in the first person. What does it mean to me to be me and what

could I wish it to mean? You must also reflect on what you regard
as your own best and most worthwhile relations with others. You
must further consider what you know or believe to be your own best
wishes and hopes for those particular persons whom you care for
most. If you will attend to yourself in relation to these other individuals who matter to you and to others who matter to you in relation
to yourself, then you will have some idea of what is involved in
being a person.

At least you will have the opportunity of forming some such idea.
You may find that you do not have the courage or the will to let this
idea of what is involved in being a person come to any clarity in
your consideration and awareness. But this will be so, if it is so,
precisely because what is involved in being a person is intrinsically
and self-authenticatingly valuable. And that which is valuable and
seen to be so is, as such, a source of demand or claim upon us. It
may be, therefore, that we refuse to admit any clear recognition of
what is involved in being a person because we wish to reject the
claims which being a person in relation to persons makes upon us. If
this is your case, then in your very refusal to admit any understanding of what I am talking about in claiming a universal concern for
persons there is contained some understanding of that claim and its
justness.

It may be, on the other hand, that all this talk about concern for
persons seems exaggerated and sentimental. We may all of us be
moved to think at some time in our lives that being a person and
being in relation to persons is of supreme importance. But to claim
that a concern for persons as persons is, and must be, the central and
universal ground for our approach to life is to fail to recognize the
way in which so much in human affairs distorts and frustrates the
development of persons. In particular, it is to ignore that there are
good grounds for holding that each and every human being has built
in as part of his or her personality elements which work against the
production of a rounded and fulfilled personalness—either in the
individual as a person or in those other persons with whom the
individual has to do. But here I would seek to call attention to what I
would describe as the dimension, or perhaps the scale, of the frustration of personalness. It is a dimension which is tellingly illus-

trated in the literature of the Absurd or in the theatre of Despair or Indifference, and not infrequently experienced in cynicism or sensuality. All these and other forms of human reactions to what is involved in being human can be reasonably and powerfully seen as evidence of what is inherently involved in being a person, and of the value of being a person, even if the value is glimpsed only in the moment of its extinction or seen through the tragedy of its frustration. Thus I expect agreement to the claim that our concern is or must be with persons, on the ground that reflection will intuitively show the strength of this claim. Further, the claim stands even if the intuition is inhibited from its full force by a fear of what that claim, if acknowledged, would involve for him who acknowledges it. It stands also, even if the intuition is threatened with nullity by the attacks and frustration to which persons are in fact often subjected. We can still see that our concern is, or ought to be, with persons.

But can we maintain this despite the fact that we cannot define precisely what is meant by 'being a person'? By referring you to your awareness of yourself and of what it is to be an 'I', and by asking you to reflect on your relationships with those fellow human beings who matter to you most, I have been seeking to provide you with an ostensive definition of 'being a person', I have been trying to point to what is meant and indicated, although it cannot be defined. In an attempt at definition we might be inclined to say that an essential feature of being a person is a capacity to enter into, and to appreciate, reciprocal and reciprocated relationships with other human beings. But I suspect that a definition of this nature would turn out to have at least some element of circularity in it. For the relationships in question have to be *personal* ones, and not just any instances whatever of relatedness between human beings. A personal relationship is one which does justice to something peculiarly human and peculiarly worthwhile among the potentialities of our existence as men. Once one has experienced it, one can tell the difference between being treated as a person and being treated impersonally or as less than a human self. But the possibilities involved in being a person cannot be made clear from theory alone or learned from a definition. Moreover, it is clear that some human beings, never having been treated as persons, do not know what it is to be a person.

And we who, I continue to claim, do know something of what is involved in being a person, have not learnt this from our general relations with all the human beings with whom we have had dealings, nor do we easily regard every human being as such, as a person. Further, many of our casual dealings which involve other human beings are not, and probably neither can be nor need to be, personal dealings. The quality and possibility of 'personalness', if I may so put it, is something which is learnt from some particular relationships with some few human beings who treat us as persons. Thus it turns out that this universal concern for persons as persons which I am putting forward as a common and acceptable basis for our investigation into the possible strength of Christianity is neither definable nor a universal feature of the experience human beings have of one another. Rather it is learnt from certain particular relationships, and can be pointed to as an experienced reality and possibility of singular importance.

It must certainly be acknowledged that this overriding concern for persons is, looked at from some points of view, of precarious status. If it is not fully definable, or definable only in a circular way, then it is particularly vulnerable to dismissal by the narrowly matter-of-fact approach of so much current thought. It is, moreover, all the more vulnerable in that there are currently available various plausible and allegedly scientific forms of *reductionism* which can be drawn, for example, from the biological or psychological or social sciences or from combinations of them. What I have in mind are the various and repeated attempts made to show that the features of truly human living—personality, love, the awareness and pursuit of value and the like—are, in the last analysis, *nothing but* particular combinations of entities, forces and relationships which can be exhaustively studied and defined by the sciences in question as their techniques and information become progressively more refined. The strength of one or more of these cases for reducing the phenomena of human personality to realities which are the proper subject matter of a necessarily deterministic science is well known. Therefore, in seeking to take as an agreed starting point a concern for persons as persons, I am asking for the acceptance as real and compelling of something which I admit to being not satisfactorily definable and which I acknowledge to be subject to the dissolving analysis of a great deal of weighty scientific thinking and knowledge.

Finally, if we are realistically to sustain this starting point, we must be aware that this concern for persons is not only threatened by the vagueness of indefinability and undermined by possible scientific forms of reductionism. Its existence as a matter of fundamental importance and reality is repeatedly contradicted in all human experience. It is scarcely our experience that most people most of the time are concerned to treat one another as persons in any deep or significant sense.

None the less, I continue to claim that our concern is and must be with persons. This is so because among all the uncertainties of definition, the possibilities of reductionism and the experiences of contradiction, we are able, in and through some of our relationships with some human beings, to perceive a fact and glimpse a value, or possibly, to perceive a value and glimpse a fact. This coincidence— or is it identity?—of fact and value is observed and experienced by us in the case of one or two of those empirical entities of animated flesh and blood who are known generically as human beings, but who are particularly known to us as persons with proper names of their own. He or she, father or mother, sister or brother, husband or wife, child or friend, simply exists as a particular piece of givenness. He or she is a fact. But the fact is that *this* he or she, precisely because he or she exists in his or her own particular and personal way, has a unique, intrinsic and demanding value. But this value *consists* in the fact that he or she exists as his or her own particular and personal self. It is thus, when we know some people as persons, that we are able to perceive that in persons, fact and value, existence and worth-whileness, coincide. And in perceiving this fact, which is the valuable existence of a person, we are at the same time confronted with the fact that our concern is with persons. To see what is involved in being a person is to know that here lies an inescapable concern.

But we have not even yet dealt sufficiently with the fact that this concern, although inescapable, is both unclear and precarious. We know, or can know, that because of what is involved in being a person our concern is and must be with persons. But we are not clear just what it is that is involved in being a person, nor are we clear that we are able or willing to pursue that concern properly. In this situation of uncertainty and precariousness the important point would seem to be this. We have some understanding of what it is or might be to be a person. This is sufficient to show us that in our awareness of 'personalness' we are catching glimpses of a reality which demands investigation. The demand for investigation has force in a twofold way. It is the demand of a given fact for explanation and the demand of a seen value for commitment and response. Thus in our perception of 'personalness' we are confronted with a coincidence of fact and value which shows every sign of being an identity and which requires an investigation and response proper to the reality which is perceived. It is on grounds such as these that I maintain, as I have already said (p. 3), that: 'If a man refuses to be concerned with persons in a manner which seeks to respond properly to the fact that they are persons, then he is refusing to face up to reality'. And I hope it is now clearer why I went on to say: 'By this I mean that he is failing to take account both of what is really the case and of what really matters in the case as it is'. I propose no theory and require no prior acceptance of a theory as our starting point for an investigation into the question of the strength of Christianity. I simply direct attention to the existence of our concern for persons and to the observable nature of that concern, and I insist that the existence and reality of this concern for persons is quite as much a fact to be reckoned with as are the uncertainties and precariousness to which I have also referred.

Thus I am seeking to avoid anything theoretical, and to do without any presupposed theory in looking for a reasonable and agreed starting point from which we may consider whether we should pay any attention to claims made for, and statements made about, Jesus. I think this is necessary because in our present circumstances we clearly cannot assume any widely agreed metaphysical presuppositions. But although I am trying to avoid metaphysical presuppositions, I cannot avoid raising metaphysical questions. Indeed, I am being highly metaphysical. For I am raising questions about, and seeking at least limited agreement about, what counts as 'real'. That is to say that I am asking you to consider what features of your own and other people's experience you ought to count as most weighty, as most worthy of your faith and commitment, in deciding what is really the case and what really matters in the case as it is. And my argument is that in our concern for persons we can see that we are on to an area of experienced reality which has strong claims to be treated as definitive for our decisions as reasonable human beings about what is to be counted as reality. And in so arguing I am also insisting that our decision about what is to be counted as reality must be related to both what is observed to be the case and what is judged to be worthwhile in, or in relation to, what is observed. I cannot accept the position that in the last human analysis it does not matter what is there or what is observable but that what matters is our attitude towards 'it', whatever 'it' is. To dissociate judgements of reality (= judgements about existence, about what is really there) from judgements of reality (= judgements about value, about what really matters) seems to me to be the way of withdrawal, immaturity and, in the end, madness. The fundamental question is 'What *is* there?', and *then* 'How worthwhile is it?'. And I focus attention on our concern for persons because here we are able to be aware, with more or less clarity, of the force of an area in which existence and value seem to be strongly and factually linked. There is, therefore, a very strong *prima facie* case for looking at this area of 'personalness' to which we are alerted by our concern for persons as the starting point for any investigation into any subject matter which claims to be of particular significance for us as human beings.

It is necessary to discuss and explain this at some length, as the too-ready adoption of slogans like 'Persons matter', or even 'Love is the only thing that matters', usually leads to, if it does not already stem from, sentimentality. Sentimentality is clearly worse than useless in any attempt to face up to and assess reality, for sentimentality is the determination to obscure reality in the haze of feelings which we find comfortable. For any serious investigation some much more rigorously established starting point is required. If, then, we are to start from our concern for persons, as I believe we should, we must take considerable pains to establish what it is we are talking about and where we are starting from. Since, also, we are raising questions about what is to be judged to be real we cannot avoid facing questions about the definition of 'personalness' (what is involved in this area).

We have to be concerned with claims to reduce the alleged facts of personalness to the observed facts of science. And we have to face experience which could be against personalness.

Finally, therefore, let us see where we have got to in setting forth and investigating the claim that our primary concern is, and ought to be, with persons. I have attempted to get you to see that we have a sufficient idea of what is involved in being a person and of the sort of concern which is a concern for persons. But we must also be prepared to say that there is a sense in which we do not know what is involved in being a person. Thus, we do not know how far being a person goes. That is to say we do not know what, if anything, could be properly described as the fulfilment of being a person, what are the possibilities as yet latent in human personalness, and what are all the demands which would have to be made on, and met by, men and women as persons, if men and women are to be truly and fully persons. Nor do we know what is the relation of the reality involved in being a person to other realities which we observe or encounter in the universe and in human life. Here we return to the possible reductionisms of science and the experienced contradictions of living already referred to. These possibilities and these experiences present us, as I have already suggested, with claims to reality which have to be evaluated in relation to the reality experienced through our awareness of the concern for persons.

So we have our concern for persons presenting us with the demands of a fact which is intrinsically valuable. But we do not know the full nature of the fact or the full weight of the value. Moreover, the status of the fact and the extent of the possibilities inherent in the value are threatened on two fronts. There is the claim that the facts involved in the field of personalness ought to be reduced to that type of data which is the proper subject matter of scientifically deterministic procedures. And there is the assertion that the values involved in being a person cannot survive the actual contradictions inflicted on personalness by the hard facts of the processes of the universe and of the actualities of human living.

The mystery of the fact of being a person, it is claimed, is to be reduced to the facts of the appropriate sciences. The mystery of the value of being a person, it is asserted, will succumb to the indifferent realities both of the universe as process and of human life as actually lived. And what in any case is the nature and extent of the mystery of being a person?

Let us be quite clear that to focus attention on what is involved in being a person is to raise a question quite as much as to point to a fact. But this is simply to increase our awareness of the dimensions of our concern for persons. In this concern we are made vividly aware of an area of human living, of experienced reality, which demands our investigation and commitment—investigation through commitment and commitment opening up further possibilities of investigation. In fact our experience of personalness invites us to faith, a faith which is to be put to the test of investigation and action. In our experience of what is involved in being a person in relation to other persons, we catch glimpses of a possible reality which is self-evidently worthwhile. Let us therefore see if this glimpsed reality of personalness will stand up to the threatened realities of actual human life and the observed processes of the universe. It is surely most reasonable, most valuable, most existential and most human, to put our faith in the possibilities of personalness. At any rate it is a faith which we have very strong grounds for trying out.

If there are those who have no glimmering of faith in the possibilities of personalness and no inkling of a desire to consider the possible kindling of such a faith, then with such I have, in the course of these lectures, little hope of communication. For my concern with Jesus Christ is linked in the closest possible way with *our* concern for persons. I am inviting you to undertake with me an investigation which I believe to be scientific in method, faithful in mood and human in its bearing. Two things strike me. I find myself confronted with two areas in which I believe I see particularly significant and demanding data. The first area is the area of our concern for persons. The second area is that of the things concerning Jesus. Of the first area I have sought to speak in this first lecture. The rest of the lectures are concerned with the second area and with the interaction between what is involved in our concern for persons and what is involved in the things concerning Jesus. I hope that the investigation contained in the lectures as a whole will give some demonstration that I am justified in the close linking which I find between our concern for persons and the things concerning Jesus.

I believe that the investigation to which I invite you is scientific in method, because it can be sufficiently shown that both in the area of our concern for persons and in the area of the things concerning Jesus we are confronted with data which has a *prima facie* claim to be considered as real and to be relevant to our assessment of reality. Hence we are fully entitled to investigate carefully what sort of data this can reasonably be claimed to be, and what bearing it can be said to have. We do not start from presuppositions or from theories but from what we believe to be given us, data, that which strikes us in our concern for persons and in the things concerning Jesus. The investigation is faithful in mood because, as I have sought to show, the data presented to us does seem to involve an intermingling of fact and value. Hence we are all the time concerned with that which at least looks as if it demands not merely investigation but commitment. We are investigating areas which on mere inspection can be seen to be important to us as human beings, or which at least look as if they would be important if they should turn out to be able to stand up to tests of reality. Hence they invite faith, commitment to them as real, to see if they turn out to be as real as they appear to be or as real as we would hope them to be. The way in which the investigation is human in its bearing can emerge only as it proceeds.

Hence I invite you to look at some of the things concerning Jesus, to see how far those things are related to our concern for persons. I believe that it will appear that the things concerning Jesus not only clearly tie in with our concern for persons, but have a defining and validating relevance. That is to say, that the things concerning Jesus both show us the direction in which lies the true fulfilment of the possibility and mystery of personalness, and then assure us that the fulfilment is a real possibility and promise, to be established in its reality over against, and in relation to, all the asserted realities of human life and the processes of the universe. If our concern is with persons, then Jesus is our concern.

II

Concern with Persons and Concern with Jesus

WE ARE NOW to investigate some of the things concerning Jesus with a view to demonstrating the interaction between these things and our concern for persons. As I have already said, the cumulative effect of the argument of the whole of the lectures is put forward as justifying the claim that this interaction is highly significant, indeed definitive, for our understanding of persons and of the world. But before we can proceed further in our overall inquiry, it is clearly necessary to give some account of why I select the particular things concerning Jesus that I do and to give some indication of what the status of these 'things' is. That is to say, I must first of all explain my decision to focus attention on the assertions made about, and the claims made for, Jesus which I am about to discuss. Then, secondly, I must give my grounds for holding that the assertions and claims under discussion can either be, or point towards, data which is relevant and weighty for determining the status of our concern for persons now. This is clearly necessary, as I am drawing material for this and the next two lectures from certain developments in Christian thinking about Jesus which took place in the first five centuries of the existence of Christianity and the Christian Church. Why then do I select what I do within that period, and how can I maintain that thinking within that period which is so remote from ours, not so much in time as in its whole manner of looking at the world, is of weight for us now?

I am going to discuss and make use of three types of statement made about Jesus or claimed to be based on things about Jesus. The first type comprises those which make use of various facets of thought about the Logos current in the first three centuries of the Christian era to make statements about the universal significance of Jesus. Then I shall turn to the implications of the discussion about the status of Jesus which took place in the fourth century in connection with the teaching of Arius and the Arians. Finally, I shall be considering the fifth century discussion in the Church about the relation of the divine in Jesus to the human in him. Clearly the topics chosen are a specialized selection from all the possible topics about Jesus which might be considered. Equally clearly, I shall be highly selective even within the material of the selected topics themselves. So it is very necessary to make clear my criteria of selection. It is quite simple. I have chosen those features of those topics within the sum total of the things concerning Jesus which appear to me to be most directly relevant to our current concerns and our current predicament with regard to persons and the significance of personalness. As I discuss the material, I shall endeavour to give some hints of the bearing which it has on this concern and this predicament. But it will not be until the second half of the lectures that I shall seek to demonstrate clearly what this bearing is. Thus, at this stage, I can only declare my criterion and explain the principle of my working method. Whether the criterion has been properly applied and whether the method leads to any positive results can appear only as the whole argument proceeds.

This matter of the working method is most important. It is necessary to make it clear that I am asking for a sustained effort in experimental thinking and I am directing attention to some examples of earlier experimental thinking which I believe I can show to be helpful and important to us now in the sort of thinking which we are compelled to do, and which we would wish to do, about persons. I direct attention back to earlier experimental thinking arising out of the things concerning Jesus because I believe that we shall find help here in our task of deciding what now we are to find 'thinkable' about the world, about ourselves, about personalness. I see no reason to succumb to the insidious plea that we must think what is 'thinkable'. Rather I retain the belief that one of the challenges of being a human being is that we are faced with the opportunity of deciding what we ought to think. If men had accepted what their generation found thinkable, we should have had no science and precious little humanness. Nor do I see why we should succumb to the arrogant complacency of assuming that what we may call 'the modern world-view' is a final and decisive arbiter of what we, as men and human beings, can or ought to think. When it comes to attempting to decide what and how we ought, responsibly and humanly, to think, there is more data than that which counts as data on some understandings of the scientific method. At least that is my contention, and I am issuing an invitation to join with me in putting this contention to the test. But I must stress that this does call for a 'sustained effort in experimental thinking' and I am aware that readiness to enter on such a sustained effort calls in itself for an act of faith.

The act of faith called for is not a consciously or explicitly Christian one. It simply involves readiness to believe that there are areas of human experience and avenues of human knowing which are worth exploring with openness, perseverance and hope. We do not have to know in advance what we are to be open to, nor what we are persevering for, nor what we have hope of. But we have to believe that openness, perseverance and hope are proper and, indeed, demanding possibilities for human beings, and we have to act on this belief. Such action will demand patience. We shall have to be patient in pursuing investigations far enough to allow the course of the investigation to disclose whether or not it is fruitful. We must not impatiently foreclose an avenue of investigation by premature and *a priori* decisions that it cannot be 'relevant' or that it demands an attitude of mind which is 'unthinkable'. We are engaged in inquiring how we should think, and what is given to us that is relevant to us, and what that relevance means for us. We are, in fact, refusing to believe, until we are compelled to believe it, that human beings are inevitably shut up within any concept of what is 'thinkable' or what is 'relevant' whatever.

I have, therefore, selected the particular things concerning Jesus which I have, precisely because I believe it can be shown that they both strengthen and inform this belief in the open possibilities which are involved in being a human being. The selection of data which is believed to be relevant to the hypothesis which one hopes to establish is, surely, a permissible, indeed a necessary, part of any valid experimental investigation. It is, however, necessary to labour this point in connection with our own particular investigation, because in what would be more normally called a scientific investigation, it would by no means be so evident that faith of some sort, perhaps of various sorts, was presupposed. In fact, the most rigorous of scientific investigations is based on presuppositions which involve faith both in the sense of an unproved decision about the way things really are and in the sense of a commitment to try out that decision in practice. But we are not here concerned to pursue further the question of the true basis of the scientific method and its presuppositions. What I am concerned to establish here is that it must not be pre-judged that my decision to select our concern with personalness and then to select certain topics within what I am calling 'the things concerning Jesus' and to juxtapose these two sets of selected material is itself nothing but prejudice.

My selection certainly involves faith in the possibilities of personalness *and* faith in the significance of the things concerning Jesus. But I have tried to show in the first lecture that faith in the possibilities of personalness is based on a reasonable judgement and is a worthwhile commitment. I am hoping to go on to show in the rest of the lectures that faith in the things concerning Jesus is at least reasonable and worthwhile in the same sense. And I am now engaged in arguing that setting up and carrying out an investigation which involves faith as a presupposition is not inevitably a prejudiced operation but is indeed the only way of proceeding with any sort of valid investigation at all. You have to believe that the area which you are investigating is worth investigating. Only the investigation itself will show whether this is so, i.e. whether your faith is strengthened, redirected or destroyed.

Further, this particular investigation is a particularly delicate and complex one because it involves questions about the fundamental nature of, and possibilities in, human life and the universe at large. Perhaps one needs a great deal of faith, which will seem to some people overwhelming stupidity, to undertake such an investigation at all. For the investigation raises questions about what is really real, what is truly true, what counts as data and what the data is good for. Some people hold that such questions cannot be proper questions. To them one must say that the investigation is precisely about whether they are proper questions or not, for the investigation is concerned with inquiring into whether we have evidence to help us in answering such questions. In fact the whole laborious paraphernalia of these lectures so far, with their tiresome refusal to get on with anything, is designed to show that the question of what is a proper question must be kept open to investigation. Or to put the matter less linguistically and more obviously metaphysically, I have been concerned to argue that it is neither scientific nor human to decide in advance where reality and value truly lie, nor to accept uncritically any presuppositions about what is thinkable as having closed the question of the limits within which we may properly think.

It should not occasion surprise that the opening lectures of what is formally a course of lectures on christology should be given over to discussion of methods of investigation and that this discussion should reveal that what is involved is an investigation into our understanding of such difficult and slippery concepts as reality, truth, humanity, personalness. For the scandal of the Christian claim (which Christians at any rate in earlier ages have believed to be the glory of the Christian gospel) has been that it has been asserted that at the heart of the things concerning Jesus there is the truth which is Jesus, and that this truth is declaratory of, and definitive of, what is lasting in reality, what is fully worthwhile in value, what is abiding in truth, what is possible for humanity and what is fulfillable in personalness. But we cannot in our present climate of opinion argue about this directly because we are prevented from getting to the scandal that such a claim should be made, or such a gospel preached *about Jesus*, rather than about some other person or some other philosophy. For it is a much more immediate scandal in most of our modern thinking that one should claim to be able, still more to be obliged, to speak at all about such things as abiding reality, ultimate value, or the fulfilment of personalness.

Therefore, I have to make it clear that I know that I am making what may well appear to be an arbitrary selection of material from an unpromising field in order to tackle questions which may well be thought to be either nonsensical or not able to be answered. I hope that the foregoing argument has sufficiently shown my grounds for proceeding in this manner. My further hope is that the subsequent argument will show that the undertaking is neither as nonsensical nor as impracticable as it may seem. I shall return in Lectures V and VI to this question of presuppositions about our understanding of reality as a whole, and there demonstrate that we cannot escape questions about what is universally valid or significant, i.e. questions about the nature of reality. I shall then direct your attention to the fact that one's presuppositions or decisions about the nature of reality practically affect one's existential and immediate approach to the situations and problems involved in being human. And I shall show conversely that one's existential approach to being human implies a judgement about the 'real nature of things'. In other words, I shall argue that the history of ideas makes it clear that we cannot escape taking or implying a universal view of things and that it is sheer escapism to pretend otherwise. This argument will reinforce my case for having considered in the first place the possible universal significance of the concern for persons, and for directing your attention to areas in the things concerning Jesus which have to do with the universal significance of Jesus.

But having explained my method and criterion of selection, as the best way of giving them a working justification, I have still to put forward my grounds for holding even experimentally and tentatively that among the things concerning Jesus discussed and asserted in the first five centuries of the Christian Church there can be that which will be useful to us now as data in deciding what is thinkable about man, the world and reality. Here again my answer can be partial only. What I have to do is to explain why I have a case for starting from where I do. Whether I turn out to have made a false start or not can appear only from the course and completion of the whole investigation. I hold that the discussions concerning Jesus in the first five Christian centuries may well provide data for guiding us in our present judgements for the following reasons.

It can be shown that the questions which were then discussed in terms of the things concerning Jesus are the same questions as now confront us, about how we are to understand our human existence in the face of the processes of the universe and in the face of what actually happens in human lives, both individually and corporately. It can at least do us no harm to consider what predecessors of ours, under conditions very different from ours, made of these questions. The very difference of their view-point might provide some stimulating, and possibly corrective, cross-checking on the way we now look at these questions, and so help us to escape from complete abandonment to subjectivism and relativism.

Further, we are surely entitled to ask ourselves whether our own whole way of looking at things has not settled down into a mythology, an accepted frame of ideas, a taken-for-granted way of looking which is, in its own way, as limited and as limiting as those frames of reference which we have now become accustomed to refer to as the mythology of earlier ages. Why not, therefore, challenge one mythology with another, i.e. confront the assumptions of the twentieth century with the formulations of the first to the fifth, when it can be shown that both are concerned with the same human questions? This would seem the more likely to be a fruitful confrontation if it should turn out to be the case that on the one hand, the formulations of the early centuries contain the germs both of our concern for personalness and of much of our scientific approach to the universe, while on the other, our twentieth-century assumptions are permitting personalness and humanness to be placed in jeopardy. It will be the task of lectures V and VI to argue this latter point, after, I hope, lectures III and IV have established the former.

But the nub of the case for pressing this investigation with material drawn from the first five Christian centuries is that the topics we shall consider demonstrate the dominating influence in those centuries of the things concerning Jesus, and therefore bear witness to the creative impact of Jesus on the thought and human understanding of that time. We shall be considering how men felt obliged to understand their life in the world and in the universe in which they lived, as a result of their acceptance of certain things concerning Jesus as decisive data. The case for taking their thought seriously, and investigating the possible interaction between their thought and ours, lies here. They acted and investigated on the faithful assumption and commitment that Jesus was a given focus and source of material for forming their views about human life and for directing their responses to, and actions in, the situation of human living. They acted on the assumption that in, and in connection with, Jesus they had data of decisive importance about the true facts and the real values of human life. What I wish to do is to investigate the nature, the basis and the bearing of this understanding.

I claim that this is an interesting thing to do in any case because a confrontation of two worked-out mythologies through some consideration of their working-out may well prove fruitful. I suggest further that it may well prove an urgently desirable thing to do in view of the fact that certain understandings of personalness and humanity which arose out of, and in connection with, the assumptions about Jesus are now threatened. And I argue still further that those assumptions of the early Christian thinkers have a claim upon the consideration of any man who has a mind which is humanly and scientifically open to the possibilities of significant evidence arising anywhere out of the givenness either of the universe or of history.

This claim arises because the basis of the dominating influence of the things concerning Jesus in the period we have to consider was held to lie in the fact that the creative impact of Jesus arose out of his historical existence and rôle. We are not dealing with cosmic and anthropological speculations which take in Jesus, we are confronted with beliefs about the world and man *based on Jesus*. At least that is the claim built into the experimental thinking which we are to study. And that is the main interest of this thinking for me, and the reason why I juxtapose it with our concern for persons as a possible source of data for our understanding of human life in the universe.

For I believe this thinking can be shown to be truly experimental thinking in that the conclusions reached or the faith held concerning man, the world and God was never determined by what the Christian thinkers had hitherto found 'thinkable'. Rather they allowed the theories which they had taken for granted as established in the thinking of the non-Christian world to be challenged, corrected and even in some way determined by what they held to be the truth of the things concerning Jesus. Thus they treated these things concerning Jesus as highly significant experimental data and this they did because they believed that at least the basis of the things concerning Jesus had been given in history in the actual life and rôle of Jesus.

In investigating our concern for persons we find that we are confronted with a given reality or given realities which have weight enough to challenge any theory which pretends to delimit for us what is 'thinkable' or to determine for us how we are to understand the universe and our place in it. This is the argument of my first lecture and it may be put in the form of the question, 'Why should we allow anything other than that which we perceive in, and experience through, our concern for persons to determine our understanding of reality, in the sense both of that which is in fact the case and in the sense of that which is truly worthwhile?' As we consider *this* question, then, I suggest that we should also consider how the things concerning Jesus were understood by the Christians of the early centuries to work in exactly the same way. That is to say, they received the things concerning Jesus as likewise weighty enough both in their factual status and in their value demand to require them to treat that which was given in connection with Jesus as determining data for their understanding of the total context of their living in the universe—of which one feature was that Jesus had lived and played a certain rôle in it. I am trying the experiment of juxtaposing the *prima facie* claim to universal significance exposed through our concern for persons with the historically made claim for the universal significance of Jesus. This I do because I believe it to be the case that our present comprehension of the concern for persons received its initial shaping from the Christian understanding of the universal significance of Jesus. I further believe it to be the case that it is a proper and renewed understanding of the universal significance of Jesus which saves and fulfils our concern for persons. And I am attempting the experiment of these lectures to see if this can, indeed, be shown.

But before I can proceed to the examination of the early experimental thinking I must endeavour by way of conclusion to this lecture to clarify what I mean by, for example, talking of 'that which was given in connection with Jesus' or by making claims based on the life and rôle of Jesus. That is to say, I am obliged to try and state a clear position on the whole vexed question of historicity and mythology. My position is that the things concerning Jesus have a strong claim to be treated as weighty data for our understanding of man and the world because at their heart and as their foundation there lies the creative impact of the actual historical Jesus. I reject the notion that the things concerning Jesus are through and through nothing but ideas which men formed to constitute a cluster of interpretations more or less loosely connected with, or occasioned by, the historical figure designated by the name-phrase 'Jesus of Nazareth'.

The most reasonable and likely conclusion, I believe, is that the impact of Jesus portrayed in the New Testament and the interpretation of Jesus put forward in the New Testament arose because, by and large, Jesus was the sort of man who actually lived the sort of life and died the sort of death which, under the conditions of Palestine in his time, would validly give rise to the impact portrayed, and the interpretations put forth, by the New Testament writers. That is to say I hold that the most valid and probable historical judgement about the New Testament is that the major constitutive event or events in its creation was, as a matter of fact, the creative living, teaching and dying of Jesus of Nazareth, and that the historical reality of the personality of Jesus is validly and effectively reflected in the New Testament writings.

My grounds for this judgement are fourfold. Firstly, when I reflect on such works of New Testament scholarship as come my way, and reflect also on my actual experience of men and communities, I do not find the thesis of the community as the primary creative force in the construction of the things concerning Jesus by any means the most credible hypothesis. It seems to me much more credible and rational to postulate an actual historical Jesus commensurate with the interpretations and responses of the community as the prior given and creative cause of the community understanding and faith. I judge that the records as they stand require an historical creative personality before they will permit of a creative responsive community.

I am, secondly, emboldened in this judgement by reflecting on the nature of the presuppositions involved in the vast mass of modern

New Testament study concerning historicity, what can be judged to have happened in history and what can be counted as plausibly historical. All these assumptions are those of the current modern mythology about the nature of the world, of reality and of human understanding. If there is a case at all for supposing, or even trying out the hypothesis, that the things concerning Jesus can constitute evidence for shaping our view of the world and man, then we are not required to succumb before we start our investigation to the presuppositions of any world-view. I am, at least, entitled to point out that in our judgements about what is or can be historical and therefore in our judgements about the most credible explanation of the New Testament evidence about Jesus we are already bringing our presuppositions to bear. When, therefore, one is engaged in questioning presuppositions, one is entitled to claim that full weight should be given to the *prima facie* evidence for the creative historical personality of Jesus *before* one starts to trim that evidence to what it is alleged is required by the modern understanding of what is historically possible or plausible.

Thirdly, I think it necessary to take account of the attitude of those who presented the evidence in the first place. It seems to me that whatever may be the form of the mythology, if it be such, in which they clothed and expressed their understanding of what they had set out, it is clear that the whole self-understanding of their faith and impact of their message turned on the fact that this 'mythology' was, so to speak, pinned to reality by the historic givenness and happenedness of Jesus (cf., e.g., the 'the Word was made flesh' of John and the 'if Christ be not risen' of Paul). They may have been quite wrong, but there can be little doubt about what they thought they were doing and about what they intended to do. Thus I find that not only does the evidence of the New Testament as a whole most reasonably require the historical impact of the creative personality of Jesus, but that those who bear witness to this have this as their necessary presupposition.

Fourthly, and finally, I am personally the more ready to accept the witness of the New Testament writers to the historically based nature of their understanding of Jesus because I find in practice that their writings serve to re-create in me and in relation to my own living, experiences, insights and occasions of a strengthening and life-enhancing nature which I can recognize as being analogous to, or continuous with, or even part of, experiences and insights to which they refer. Thus I have experiential grounds for holding them to be trustworthy witnesses to that of which they purport to speak.

But now I have moved fully into the realm of faith! None the less it is a faith with reasons, and I see no reason to count my own experiences as *less* valid than those of others. Further, the majority of my reasons for my position on historicity do not depend on this faith. And finally, I have, at this stage, only to give reasons which are sufficient for adopting a certain basis for a piece of experimental thinking. This basis is that the things concerning Jesus can reasonably be taken to be based on the historical creative personality of Jesus of Nazareth. So we are now ready to proceed in the next two lectures to consider the understanding of the world, God and man which was worked out in the first five Christian centuries on the basis of the things concerning Jesus. As we do so, we can reasonably entertain the belief that this is a constructive and creative understanding of the realities of the world and of man's situation in the world, built up from the realities of Jesus' life in the world and the realities of the life-experience and understanding of the early Christians. We are not, therefore, to consider what are simply theories or ideas of the world. We are to consider interpretations which have a claim to be taken seriously in *their* claim that they are based on given historical and experiential evidence. Alongside our glimpse of the possible universal significance of our concern for persons we are to set the claimed universal significance of Jesus. The main purpose of the argument of this lecture has been to show that there is a case for holding that the claimed universal significance of Jesus is as much based on the realities experienced in human life in the world as is the claim for the universal significance of persons.

III

The Universal Significance of Jesus

WE COME NOW to considering the understanding of the world, God and man which was worked out in the first five centuries on the basis of the things concerning Jesus. The chief ground for turning our attention to this is that this understanding has, or was believed to have, a basis in facts. That is to say that the Christian understanding of God, man and the world is held to follow from the things concerning Jesus, while the things concerning Jesus are held to be based in the actual serial realities of the living and dying of the historical character known as Jesus of Nazareth. We are to examine what purports to be the effects of the impact of the historical creative personality of Jesus of Nazareth on some men's understanding of themselves and of their place in the universe.

But how was it possible for the impact of one historical personality to be decisive for a man's understanding of himself and of the world? And if and when this is made clear can it conceivably remain a plausible or persuasive possibility for us? This is what we have to investigate.

The impact of Jesus was understood as of universal significance in the first place because it occurred in a particular context, namely that of what we now call first-century Palestinian Judaism. This context provided the set of ideas about the world and the pattern of understanding life which made it possible to claim that Jesus was of universal significance. I am not, at this stage, concerned with the *validity* of this set of ideas and of this pattern of life-understanding, but with their *existence*. Further, I am not suggesting, because it would not be true to do so, that there is a precise and clear pattern that can be designated 'first-century Palestinian Judaic thought'. Even on the evidence we have, which is by no means complete, it is clear that the 'pattern' is one of great complexity and diversity—so much so that even to speak of 'the pattern' at all is to over-systematize and over-simplify. None the less, we may speak of the whole set of ideas current in first-century Palestine as the matrix which provided the concepts which made possible the identification of the universal significance of Jesus of Nazareth, or at least provided the possibility of claiming universal significance for Jesus.

Now in this whole matrix, the concept of the Messiah is clearly of fundamental importance. The first form which the claim for the universal or potentially universal significance of Jesus took was that Jesus was the Messiah, that Jesus is the Christ. For this claim to be made, two things are necessary. Firstly, that the notion of Messiah should already have a content, and secondly, that there should be things about Jesus which lead to relating that concept to his person. The notion of Messiah obtains its content from the set of thought-forms and life-understanding in which—in its turn—it has developed. And *this* context is the experience and faith of the Jewish people stretching back into the history of Israel and Judah. What the Jewish people made of this experience and history of theirs is reflected in the pages of what we now call the Old Testament.

We do not need to discuss the surely insoluble question of how much in the Old Testament is 'historical', in the sense of trying to decide, or needing to decide, whether any particular account, say of an Exodus journey, or of the reign of a particular king of Israel, provides you with data enabling you to make judgements of the 'what-you-would-have-seen-if-you-had-been-there' sort. For the purposes of my thesis we can put on one side this question about the particular historicity of particular happenings. For the essential point about the Old Testament attitude to history which is central to the content of the notion of the Messiah is this. The Old Testament portrays and reflects the development of the faith that as a matter of fact God controls history for the sake of his people. This, of course, is one of the ideas which is widely held at the present time to be an unthinkable one. It is necessary, therefore, to reiterate that I am not at present discussing validity or even 'thinkability' but simply existence as a fact in the history of ideas. I shall hope, in due course, to display my grounds for taking this idea seriously now. Meanwhile, there is no need to go into details about particular instances of the historical weightiness of the Old Testament. The fundamental point is that the Old Testament makes it clear that the Jewish view of the world which was still flourishing in the Palestine of Jesus of Nazareth had built into it the belief that the facts, events, happenings of history were susceptible of, and conformable to, a personal purpose. This purpose was personal in a twofold sense. Firstly, the serial happenings which constituted the history of the Jewish people were held to be moving, or to be capable of being moved, in a direction which fulfilled the life of the Jewish people (and perhaps the life of all men). Secondly, there was held to be a mover of the events of history towards this personal end (sc. end involving persons) who could be thought of as personal, in the sense that this mover was concerned with this personal end and to this end was concerned to enter into a reciprocal relationship with the persons involved in the end.

The concept which most conveniently focuses the Jewish understanding of the world through this understanding of the personal purposes related to history is that of the Kingdom of God. This concept is most convenient for our purposes because there can be no reasonable historical doubt that the idea of the Kingdom of God played a central part both in the thinking of Jesus and in the initial thinking about Jesus. The Kingdom of God stands for that realm in which there is finally achieved and established those purposes of God for his people which were discovered in their history and which it was believed would be worked out through their history. The Kingdom of God was the situation in which, or the state of affairs through which, God would establish everything in full accordance with the pattern of personal purpose which stemmed from his own being. This pattern was something which the Jews believed they had learnt from their experiences of their history in and through which God had made himself and his purposes known to them. To achieve this understanding and knowledge of God, they had needed the insight and discernment of inspired men, but this prophetic insight, they believed, had led to the perception of the real pattern of God's activity which was the expression of the reality of God's being. Prophetic insight had given true perception which led to real knowledge about God because that prophetic insight was itself God-given. Since it was the true pattern of the real expression of God's being which was perceived in and through their history the Jews were quite clear that this pattern would be fulfilled in the final pattern which history produced, and that they would have a real share in this pattern. It was this final pattern which was thought of and expected under the notion of the establishment by God of his Kingdom. The true pattern of the being and activity of the living God has been experienced and discovered by the Jews in and through their history. Therefore this pattern was bound to be established. God had been truly met with in history, therefore history was bound eventually, to produce God's purpose. God would establish his Kingdom.

What is important here is the structure and the internal logic of the thought and of the whole approach to the world and of the understanding of life involved in this way of thinking. The *truth* of this way of understanding the world and the life of the world is clearly not finally or decisively verifiable. The very structure of the thinking itself precludes this. For the truth of this understanding of the world is not finally and fully established until there is produced out of history that state of affairs in which everything is fully in accordance with the pattern of the being of God. But that state of affairs is the final establishment of the Kingdom of God, and the establishment of the Kingdom of God is what is confidently looked for. Therefore it is clear that this faith of the Jews that God controls history for the sake of his people, i.e. that history reflects, and is, or can be, related to, a personal purpose, is not a truth *statement*. It is not something which is based, or can be based, adequately on a demonstrable existing and observable state of affairs. But although this faith about a God active in history does not involve a truth *statement*, it is exceedingly important to notice that it does involve a truth *claim*. The Jewish faith in any form which is continuous with the internal logical structure developed in, and reflected in, the Old Testament is not to be understood as just an attitude to the world. It is an attitude to the world which has, as an integral feature of its structure, the claim that it is an attitude validly based on, and corresponding to, that reality which is both perceivable in the historical realities of this world, and also the reality which extends beyond, and ultimately determines, the realities of this world. The God whom the Jew faithfully knows and whose activity the Jew faithfully perceives is the true and living God, and therefore his Kingdom *will* come.

This truth claim which is tied into history because it is read out of history is so truly a truth claim that it led to the Jews finding their own history an acute problem. For this history showed no signs of verifying the truth of that which it was believed had been perceived in and through history. Hence the urgency in many Jewish circles of various forms of the hope of the appearance of the Messiah, of the coming of him who was appointed and anointed by God at least to initiate the coming of the Kingdom of God. Something *must* occur in the history of the Jewish people to make it clear that the God known in and through their history was the true God, i.e. truly there as God, and that the personal pattern discerned as at work in history would have its fulfilment. So acute was this problem of history, that round about what we now call the first centuries B.C. and A.D. many Jews were tending to submerge their distinctive understanding of history as at least potential material for the purposes of a God concerned with persons in syncretistic versions of the various non-biblical faiths and philosophies current at that time. The view which these faiths and philosophies took of the world and of man is something which we shall have to consider in relation to the development of the Christian understanding of these matters. At this stage it is sufficient to note that the distinctive biblical understanding of history as the sphere of the activity of a God concerned with persons and as the source of material which could be productive of personal purposes and patterns was under very great threat. What evidence was there to sustain this faith in the living God actively involved in events against the actual course of events in Judaea with its minute significance in the midst of the vastness of the Roman Empire?

Christianity arose because a small group of persons conditioned by the biblical tradition and faith which I have been describing believed that they had discovered a decisive piece of evidence, to wit that God had sent his Messiah and that the Messiah was Jesus. The basis of the discovery of the universal significance of Jesus of Nazareth lay in the identification of him as the Lord's Messiah, as the Christ of God. This had universal significance because of the understanding of the world, history and man which lay behind the Messianic expectations of the Jews. And these Messianic expectations arose because the Jews believed that they had been led to discover through their history the true pattern of the being and activity of the true God. Without this context, background and tradition no claim to the universal significance of Jesus of Nazareth could have arisen. But the claim that the Messiah *has* come because Jesus is the Messiah does not only presuppose this pattern of thought, understanding and faith. The claim that Jesus is the Messiah is also a claim that this pattern of thought, understanding and faith is valid. God is rightly and not mistakenly known as active in history for the fulfilment of a personal and purposive pattern.

Once again, therefore, we have a truth claim and not just the assertion of a particular attitude couched in a particular mythology. Moreover, we have here a truth claim which is based on what is clearly held to be a truth statement, viz. that Jesus is, as a matter of fact, the Messiah. For the discovery that this Jesus of Nazareth is the Christ is clearly understood as the recognition of a fact. It was a fact which came to be recognized as such by the cumulative effect of other observations. Jesus' conduct of his own life made it clear that he believed himself to have a mission in connection with the coming of the Kingdom of God. His teaching and actions were concerned with the nature of that Kingdom and that coming, with the presence of the power of that Kingdom, and with the response required to the coming of the Kingdom. His actions in challenging the established authorities and in following that challenge up by what became his last journey to Jerusalem, and the interpretation which he put upon the fate which threatened him during his meal with his disciples before his arrest, makes it sufficiently historically clear that he came to see his death as part of the pattern of his mission in connection with the coming of the Kingdom of God.

Thus we can have little doubt that in his self-understanding Jesus saw both his living and his dying as centrally associated with

God's bringing in of his Kingdom. So many people have found this whole complex of ideas either unthinkable or else thinkable only when it has been translated into a demythologized version which represents the modern guess at the currently acceptable categories which can most plausibly be alleged to *be* a translation of the original, that it has been claimed that the evidence for the fact that Jesus did think in this way is of the shakiest. But this is the result of a grave confusion of thought which does more credit to a misdirected respect for Jesus on the part of those who think this way, than to their powers of historical judgement. In fact, the evidence that Jesus did so understand and direct his life is quite satisfactorily strong. The difficulty is that so much turns on whether his understanding and living was justified, authentic and valid or not. Many people find it impossible to believe that the sort of question posed by the living and dying of Jesus, understood in the way in which it seems very probable that he himself understood it, can be posed at all. They therefore hold that it cannot historically be the case that he lived in such a way or understood his living in such a way. But this is simply to allow sufficiently probabilified historical data to succumb to current prejudice. '*I* cannot think like that, therefore Jesus cannot have thought like that whatever the evidence may suggest'. Such an attitude directed, say, to Napoleon or Augustus Caesar, would be immediately laughed out of court. But then one's judgement of the historical nature of the existence of Napoleon or Augustus Caesar does not necessarily affect one's judgement about the nature of historical existence as such. The difficulty clearly lies in the implications of the tradition which is the context of the life of Jesus and with which Jesus identified himself. The difficulty lies not in the shakiness of the evidence but in what the evidence might be evidence for. For what is at issue is whether there is evidence that there is a God who is active in history for the fulfilment of a personal and purposive pattern.

Jesus was recognized as such evidence because of the pattern of his living and dying seen in the context of the biblical and Jewish understanding of the world. This tradition provided a context which made the identification of Jesus or someone else as the Messiah a possibility. But it was the actual pattern of Jesus' living and dying which gave to the notion of Messiah both content and existential actuality. The recognition of Jesus as the Messiah was the recognition of a fact and the recognition of this fact anchored the biblical and Jewish interpretation of history in the sheer serial givenness of history.

But we still have to reckon with the fact that the recognition of Jesus as the Messiah did not simply arise out of the pattern of his living and dying, up to his death on a cross. The pattern of his living and dying had to place him in a Kingdom of God context and therefore within the scope of the notion of Messiahship before any recognition of him as Messiah could occur. But the relevant records indicate that Jesus was first decisively, rather than tentatively, recognized as the Messiah when a comparative handful of people among those who had been associated with him became convinced that the cross on which he had died had not terminated the pattern and the purpose of Jesus' life. Their conviction, based on evidence which they seemed to some extent to be able to share and to discuss and recognize in common, was that 'God had raised him up'. They believed they had evidence that the understanding, commitment and direction of the life of Jesus had not terminated in his death on the cross, but was continued in his livingness, known to his immediate followers and to be made known as widely as possible in the world at large.

Here again it is important to notice that this discovery of the resurrection of Jesus was taken to be the discovery of a fact. This is made sufficiently clear by the famous, or perhaps it should nowadays be the notorious, story of the empty tomb. If this story in its various versions is at all historically accurate then it reflects one of the series of events and experiences through which the discouraged followers of Jesus became persuaded that he was in fact not dead and finished, but alive and purposefully active. If this does not recount one of the events which caused belief in the Resurrection, but rather reflects the Resurrection belief in story form, then it still reflects the fact that this belief in its initial form, however it was caused, did include the claim that the Resurrection, whatever else it might be, was a fact in a series of events. Thus it is sufficiently clear, although to us no doubt unpleasingly clear, that the recognition of Jesus as the Messiah was held to be the discovery of a fact. This discovery arose out of the cumulative effect of a whole set of things concerning Jesus. These included the pattern and direction of his living and dying, together with the self-understanding displayed by Jesus and the set of experiences common within a strictly limited class of followers which added up to the recognition of the fact of the Resurrection. Thus it was proclaimed as a fact that God has raised up Jesus and so made it decisively clear that Jesus was the Messiah. This fact about Jesus was thus held to be the decisive fact in the whole world. It constituted *the* good news, that is to say the Gospel.

As I have shown, the possibility of such a truth claim being made which was at the same time a claim to universal significance could only have arisen within a tradition which had evolved such an understanding of God, the world and man as was to be found in the Judaism which expected the coming of the Kingdom of God. This was a way of looking at the world which implied the belief that it is history which produces the key to the cosmos, for history provides material in and through which the Lord God works out the pattern of his personal purposes. It was a belief which had grown up out of history and through history and had led the Jews to look *to* history. What some men in this Jewish tradition discovered was that the facts concerning the man Jesus of Nazareth led to the recognition of this man as God's Messiah, that is to say, the person in history who has the rôle of bringing God's purpose in history to its climax.

Now if we try to take a glance at the whole gamut of events which might properly be held to fall within the scope of human history, we must surely be inclined to conclude that the very notion of 'history as a whole' is an empty one and that the suggestion that history provides the material for the working out of the pattern of a personal purpose is absurd. To suggest further that one historical personage is both the vindication of the existence of this personal purpose and the definition of the nature of that purpose, is simply to put forward the absurdity of absurdities. Theoretically, that is to say looked at apart from particular facts, there would seem to be very much to be said for this view. But there are some particular facts which count obstinately against the absurdity and for the truth of this view. Firstly, there is the evolution of the Jewish understanding of the world and history through the Jews' experience of their history. Secondly, there is the pattern of the living and dying of Jesus placed within and orientated towards that understanding of the world and history. And thirdly, there is the discovery that Jesus' understanding and mission was vindicated by the fact that his dying had been superseded by his living.

But, we may feel obliged to say, the Resurrection cannot be true, cannot be a fact and cannot be discovered. *That* precisely is the question. Some people held that it was true because it was discovered to be a fact or discovered itself as a fact. Before we are quite sure that this *must* be absurd we should consider that many people today are ready to accept the Sartreian absurdity that all life and all reality is absurd. Why should the Sartreian absurdity of meaninglessness be more reasonably acceptable than the Christian absurdity of meaningfulness, especially when we consider the weight of that area of reality to which our concern for persons directs us, especially too, when the Christian gospel does not either proceed from absurdity or point to absurdity ? The Christian gospel proceeds from what can reasonably be claimed to be data thrown up within a particular historical series and focused within a particular historical life. And the Christian gospel points to an understanding of God, the world, and man which can be seen to be consistent with that openness, perseverance and hope which I have already referred to as a recognizable option in our assessment of the human situation.

I shall try to portray this direction of the Christian Gospel in some faint measure in my last two lectures. I shall argue in more detail about the conflict between meaningfulness and absurdity in my fifth and sixth lectures. I am at the moment engaged in arguing the case for giving a hearing to the claim for the universal significance of Jesus discovered to be the Christ of God and for not dismissing *a priori* the possibility of the discovery of his Resurrection. I want now to continue to investigate the weight of this claim concerning the resurrected Jesus Christ by outlining its creative effect in the understanding of God, the world and man in the centuries immediately following its first appearance. I am quite clear that we can never finally know, at any rate in this world, that Jesus is the Christ. We have no final truth statement, only a truth claim. We are, of course, investigating the Christian *faith*. But a truth claim is the more authenticated the more it can be shown to have a creative and life-enhancing effect on and through those who entertain it and assert it.

Thus we turn to consider the creative effect of accepting it as true that Jesus is the Christ.

The recognition that Jesus is the Christ means that one discovers not only that Jesus is the Christ but also that there is a Christ and he is Jesus. Thus this recognition not only establishes the actual and historical existence of the Messiah, but also defines the nature and content of this existence. We have an ostensive definition of Messiahship which at the same time reinforces and establishes the historical relevance and involvement of the whole way of looking at the world which had produced the historical expectation of the historical appearance of the Messiah. So the discovery that this particular Jesus of Nazareth is the Messiah reinforces that understanding of the world which sees history as providing the material for the working out of the pattern of the purposes of a personal God. Hence there is a working vindication of the belief that history produces the key to the cosmos and an essential reinforcement of the faith that *this* attitude to the world is a truthful response to the way things really are, to the ultimate and decisive nature of reality. But, further, as there is an actually lived out pattern of the life of Jesus, we have in his historical personality the pattern of the key to the cosmos. To discover that this Jesus is the Christ is to discover the fact that is determinative of one's understanding of all other facts. (It is *not* a fact which allows us to deny or ignore other facts; the escapism in the face of facts which Christians in practice tend to share with other human beings is to be discussed later.)

This determining nature of the existence of Jesus for the understanding of, and approach to, all existence is the central implication of the recognition of Jesus as the Christ, but it was an implication which had to be realized, sustained and then creatively maintained over against, and in fruitful relationship with, the current world-understandings of the world in which Christianity came to life.

The structure of the development of this implication of the discovered fact that Jesus is the Christ can be seen in the sequence of affirmations about Jesus which gradually became systematized in the course of the first five centuries. Alongside the discovery that Jesus is the Christ there arises the affirmation that Jesus is Lord. The term 'Lord' used in this context has, naturally, a complex history of its own. But this we need not study, for it is sufficiently clear that the statement 'Jesus is Lord' is logically a translation of 'Messiah' into a term which has the possibility of a much wider understanding than the Jewish term, even in its Greek form Christ. Thus 'Jesus is Lord' means that Jesus is the determining fact concerning the proper understanding of existence in the world and in history.

But this proper understanding includes the reinforcement of the discovery that history produces the key to the cosmos. Hence the affirmation 'Jesus is Lord' demands that the Christian understanding of the cosmos shall both fight with, and come to terms with, all other understandings of the cosmos. In the first five centuries this dialogue which is also a battle, and conflict which is also a creative construction, focuses on the further affirmation that Jesus is the Logos. Jesus is the key to the understanding of the cosmos, of the realm of things, as well as to the understanding of history, the realm of persons, *and the understanding of these two realms must be united*. It is here that the real battle was fought in the fourth and fifth centuries and it is here, as I hope to show in the second half of the lectures, that the real battle is still being fought.

How are we to understand our human situation? Is it the realm of things, the proper subject matter of a deterministic science, which finally defines reality? Or is it the realm of persons with possibilities, even in history, of openness, perserverance and hope? Or must we conclude that, for the sake of personalness, we have to have one approach to the realm of things and another to the realm of persons and that there can be no constructive reconciliation between them? That is to say, must we affirm personalness in the face of the fact that reality as a whole is ultimately absurd? It is to the fourth and fifth century version of this debate that I shall devote my next lecture. The debate took the form of a debate about the status of Jesus. But, as I shall show, this debate was not at all a series of metaphysical mystifications. It was a debate which was about what are our questions too. For on the basis of the things concerning Jesus, Christianity opposes the view that it is nature and not history, the realm of things and not the realm of persons, which ultimately determines reality. Christianity also opposes the view that, in the end, reality is absurd.

IV

God, Man and the World – and the God-Man

TO DISCOVER THAT Jesus is the Christ is to discover the fact that is determinative of one's understanding of all other facts. This is the universal significance of Jesus which follows from the events of his living, dying and Resurrection. For these events identify Jesus as the historical personality upon whom and through whom there is focused the personal purposes of the God who is active to bring out of the stuff of history the pattern of personal fulfilment. Thus, if Jesus is the Christ, then Jesus is Lord, the personal existence who is significant not only for Jews who expect a Messiah to vindicate the meaning of history, but also for Gentiles, whatever expectation or lack of it their particular world-views encourage. For as the Christ has appeared as an actual historical existence, the belief that history produces the key to the meaning of existence in the world has been vindicated. So the factual and historical existence of Jesus Christ claims a determining significance for all men's understanding of the cosmos. This is the meaning asserted for the existence of Jesus Christ because it is the meaning implied by the existence of Jesus Christ. We have now to consider how this meaning of the givenness of Jesus Christ made its way and unfolded its further implications in engagement with men's understandings of their existence in the world of the Graeco-Roman civilization of the second to fifth centuries.

Both Jews and Greeks had evolved a belief that man in his peculiar humanness and the universe in its peculiar givenness either did essentially fit together or were ultimately capable of being fitted together. To have a belief that man and the universe fit together is to imply a presupposed understanding that it sometimes makes sense to set men and the universe over against one another. Seeing that 'the universe' ought to mean 'everything there is' and men must be included in 'everything there is', it seems odd that it should ever make sense to set 'men' and 'the universe' over against one another. But this is really to try to use a logical quibble to step aside from an existential problem. It is clear enough that men have found and do find the world a problem. That is to say they find that their existence in the world is a problem to themselves. The universe, in the sense of everything there is, is constantly posing problems to men in their humanness. Men find that the things which matter to them are swept aside, disturbed, frustrated by 'things in general'. We are here back to the problems which I discussed in my first lecture, when I referred to those things in our understanding of the world and of the life in the world which count against, or work against, our awareness of the supreme importance of the things concerning personalness. We are back also to the question of the Absurd which is indeed the same question. Man finds his existence in the world a problem to him. Is there an answer to this problem? Do men and the universe fit together? In our discussion of this during the second half of the lectures, we shall be considering mainly the way Western thought has developed on this problem, but we shall clearly have to consider also what may be called the Oriental suggestion that the problem is to be solved by learning how to transcend and ignore it. The solution lies in losing the problem by realizing that the problem is an illusion created by the illusion of desire for an answer. At present, however, we must confine our attention to the historical development of Christian thinking in its early setting.

Christianity, then, made its way in a world which was heir to two major ways of thinking about how men and the universe fitted together. The Jews believed that the tie-up occurred in and through history, because history provided the material out of which God produced the pattern of his purpose which was concerned with the fulfilment of persons. Men and universe fitted together because God so fitted them. God is thought of as the Creator who is responsible for the beginning of the universe, the Judge who is responsible for the end, and the Saviour who can be relied upon to take such action as will ensure the achievement of his personal purposes. An expression of this understanding of things is to be found in the looking for the Kingdom of God and the hope of the coming of the Messiah which we have discussed at length in the previous lecture. The tie-up between things as they are and what men require for their fulfilment occurs through history because God can be relied upon to bring about this tie-up.

The main answer to this problem in the tradition of Greek thinking was rather different. The tie-up between man and the universe did not occur through the activity of God, it was a fact because of the existence of rationality. The faith here was not a developing faith in God but a pre-supposed faith in reason. The universe *was* a universe, a whole which could be thought about coherently and *as* a whole because it was ordered. It had, basically, harmony and pattern, and therefore unity. It was, in fact, the *cosmos*, the ordered and comprehensible whole. Now that which on the one hand produces an ordered and patterned whole and on the other hand appreciates order and pattern, is reason, which is precisely concerned with order, measurement and pattern.

There was one common word for reason, both in the sense of that basic ordering of the universe which made understanding possible, and in the sense of the human capacity to arrange matters in order and so to understand. The same word, too, was used of the speech which both formulates and conveys meaning. This word was *logos*. Man and the universe fitted together because of the *logos* of the *cosmos*. The universe had an underlying essential and rational unity. Man had an essential affinity with this ordering rationality of the universe by virtue of his reason, which was what distinguished him from every other existing thing. And by the ordered and ordering exercise of his reason, man could lay bare his essential affinity with the universe and live in harmony with it and in it. This understanding of the way man and the universe fitted together took on various forms, from the immanentism of the Stoics to the transcendentalism of the Platonists, but we have time to consider only the basic structure of the understanding. The Jew, whether or not he had come to give reason a part to play in his understanding of the world, put his faith in God. The Greek, whether or not he believed in God, put his faith in reason.

At the time when Jesus of Nazareth was born and in the subsequent years, the Jewish faith worked up to an acute historical crisis with the final capture of Jerusalem by the Romans in A.D. 70 and the final abortive revolt of the second century. Among some, the Jewish faith in God survived triumphantly, but the hope of history and the hope in history lay quiescent as far as the general history of Western thought about the world went until we come to such a secularized form as Marxism. (Here is a line of inquiry which we cannot now pursue.) Others among the Jews became so disillusioned in their whole faith through the actual course of historical events, that they abandoned all belief in the God of their fathers as a God who in any sense tied together the affairs and events of this world and the true concerns of men. Such Jews shared in, and contributed to, the growth of a very widespread and variegated religious development which is characteristic of the climate of thought in which Christianity developed, and which is known generally as Gnosticism.

The sources of the particular forms of Gnosticism are as various as are the many religions and philosophical systems which were to be found flourishing in the Roman and Hellenistic civilizations which existed round the Mediterranean and stretched as far East as the Indus. But we are concerned only with the basic structure of the common answer which all these forms gave to the problem of man and the world. This answer took the shape which it did, and gained the currency which it did, because of the collapse of the Greek faith (if I may be allowed so to call it for ease of reference) in reason, which was, of course, far more widespread and general than the Jewish faith in God. We shall, therefore, now confine our attention to the development of the Christian understanding of the things concerning Jesus in relation to the problems posed by the world-understandings current in Graeco-Roman thought, and shall no longer be concerned with the development in Judaism. In thus turning aside from Judaism, we shall not only be following the course of historical development, we shall also be following out the logic of the discovery that Jesus is the Christ. For if Jesus is the Christ, then the future of the living understanding of the way in which God uses history as material for the production of the pattern of his personal purposes lies in its main stream with the things concerning Jesus, and not with Judaism which has failed to identify the fact of facts, viz., that the Messiah *is* Jesus.

I refer to this turning aside from Judaism in this rather pointed way so that it may be quite clear that the logic of the things concerning Jesus does involve what many people hold to be the scandalously offensive claim that these things hold a decisive key to the proper understanding of man's existence in the universe. Nothing is to be gained by concealing this scandalous fact, for it arises from the very particularity, concreteness and historicity of the basis of the things concerning Jesus. *This* data and no other is finally decisive for our true understanding of man and the world. Since it is the thesis of these lectures that it is here that the very strength of Christianity lies, I can scarcely be expected to conceal it, even if the claim involves a scandal which constitutes a particular obstacle to the acceptance of the claim. I would just ask once again for suspension of judgement and openness of mind. Let us follow the way the claim works before we reject it *a priori*. Further, I hope to show in the last two lectures how the exclusiveness of the claim of Christianity is to be related to a way of life whose aim is total openness.

Christianity, therefore, as heir to the Jewish hope of history and in history, enters upon a world in which there is less and less belief that man and the universe fit together. In the complexity and vastness of the Roman Empire, men had found it more and more difficult to believe that the underlying pattern of things was reasonable or that men could, by the use of their reason alone, penetrate to any unchanging pattern of existence beyond the complexity and perplexity of the change and decay in the midst of which they lived. The very orderliness and unchangingness of the heavens which had once seemed evidence of the celestial harmony of the cosmos to be enjoyed by reason had somehow taken on the aspect of a relentless and implacable fate which maintained all the processes and events of the universe in a fixed order which had no concern with or place for personal development and fulfilment. Moreover, society had become too mixed, changing and large for men to find themselves at home in a manner which could give them any confidence that things in general had any room for their particular personal concerns. The various philosophical ways which had once been thought of as ways to answering the problem of existence in the discovery of abiding truth were still followed, but generally without much serenity or assurance. For many, especially in the big cities, such ways were in any case above them, so they turned to any cult which had a sufficient veneer of philosophy to look like an answer, or to any mythology of one tradition or another which looked religiously authoritative. Here men sought to find a revealed answer to the problem of their existence which would lift them out of their homelessness in an alien universe, and give them the opportunity to come to terms with the conditions of their own existence, in a way productive of peaceful and hopeful living. Everywhere and at every level of sophistication and credulity there was a search for Gnosis, for the knowledge which would tell a man where he came from, what was his true end, and how, in the midst of the existence thrust upon him, he could find his way to the true end by escaping from the alienation of his actual existence to the fulfilment of his essential being.

By virtue of their common feature of claiming to offer this saving knowledge (*gnosis*), the vast range of philosophies, theosophies, cults and magical systems which developed at this time are given the generic name of Gnosticism. They had, as I have already suggested, a basic structure to the answer which they gave to the problem of man and the world. Both the world and history were to be despaired of. Reality is essentially dualistic. The true spiritual reality of man has somehow got mixed up with, and trapped in, a world of matter and a series of events to which his essential self is wholly alien. If there is any hope for man at all it must lie in a complete escape from the alien matter of history and the indifferent, or more likely positively malignant, matter of the cosmos. It is because of this dualistic despair of both the universe and history that Gnosticism constitutes the meeting point of the Jew disillusioned with history, the Greek disillusioned with reason, and the Oriental who never believed that man and the cosmos fitted together in any case.

But Christianity had arisen with the discovery that Jesus was the Christ and therefore was committed to a reinvigorated and redefined view of history as the sphere of the working out of a personal purpose and, as such, productive of the key to the cosmos. Hence the discovery made in and through a Jewish context that Jesus was the Christ had to be translated into the more widely comprehensible claim that Jesus Christ was Lord, definitive of any man's understanding of history and the cosmos.

In maintaining and developing their understanding of Jesus Christ as Lord within the sort of context which I have been very briefly describing in my discussion of Gnosticism, Christians of the second century found themselves picking up a Greek notion which was still viable, although it was no longer an unchallenged axiom of thought. This notion was that men and the universe fit together because of the Logos of the cosmos. Men had sought through many philosophical channels to become clear about and to respond to the Logos. But it was Christians who had found him, or rather, been found by him. Jesus Christ is the Logos of the cosmos.

To make such an assertion two things are required. Firstly, there must be the discovery that Jesus Christ is given as definitive of our understanding of the world and of our place and hope in it. I have sketched out the structure of the way in which this discovery arose. Secondly, there must be in existence a way of looking at the world and of understanding man's place in the world which gives content to the notion of 'the Logos of the cosmos'. I have *very* briefly sketched out the structure of the background to this notion. Now this second notion clearly reflects what men at some period found thinkable. Indeed it actually sums up the structure of their thinking. It was a very widely taken-for-granted notion and authoritative as such. Thus it represents one of the then currently respectable cosmic intuitions or cosmic myths. Men assumed that the universe was in some sense rational, i.e. tied up with the distinctive humanness of human beings. Or else they believed that it was, or hoped that it was, or feared that it was not. For, as I have already indicated, this way of looking at the world was, in the first centuries of our era, under heavy threat, or actually abandoned by many. None the less, it made sense to search for the Logos of the cosmos. It represented a comprehensible, a thinkable view of the world which could, therefore, be asserted or denied in a meaningful way.

The second and third century development of the Logos doctrine in connection with the things concerning Jesus is typical of the pragmatic manner in which Christian thought develops. This development might be called accidental. I would maintain that it should properly be called experimental, proceeding by means of the various groups of data available and thereby finding out what the data is good for. In the definitive witness to the things concerning Jesus which had crystallized out into what we call the New Testament, the *term* 'Logos' had been used by the writer of the Fourth Gospel to express his insight that Jesus was definitive of both history and cosmos because of his role in relation to the Old Testament understanding of God and the world. He prefaces his gospel with an introduction which makes use of this term (whose English translation is usually given as *Word*) in such a way as to make it clear that he is aware that the term 'Word' both fits into biblical and Jewish talk about God, the world and history, and has the chance of fitting into Greek talk about the world and rationality. In prefacing his exposition of the things concerning Jesus with the sentence 'the Word became flesh' the author is making use of a creative insight into the implications of the discovery that Jesus is the Christ. It is an insight which serves as the basis for a tying together of the Jewish understanding of the world with the Greek understanding of the cosmos in a new and creative synthesis which is stimulated by and based on the things concerning Jesus.

The Christian apologists of the second and third centuries developed this insight much further for, for reasons which I have sketched, the pressing questions of their time forced them to be concerned with the cosmic significance of the things concerning Jesus. As one now studies the way in which they developed their arguments about Jesus Christ as the Logos of the cosmos, it becomes very clear that the term 'Logos' was so useful precisely because it was a very ambiguous one. The *term* appeared in the Greek version of the Old Testament, in the preface to the Fourth Gospel, and in various philosophical contexts with Platonic, Stoic and other flavours. But, of course, it operated with different meanings in the different contexts precisely because the different contexts were differing ways of looking at the world. Thus it often seems that theology proceeds by puns. For example, the Jew is desperately concerned with the Word of God (Greek: *Ho Logos tou theou*). The Stoically inclined Greek, say, is much concerned to live according to the rational shape of the cosmos (Greek: to live—*kata ton Logon*). Call Jesus Christ the Logos and you have satisfied the Jew and excited the Greek. But it really all is a matter of words, of a convenient pun.

My point is that this is not so. Rather, given that Jesus is the Christ and therefore the definitive fact for the human understanding of both history and cosmos, then the second and third century apologists had every reason for expressing this and exploring the implications of this in the language of the cosmic intuitions, of the world-understandings, of their time. But the decisive question was whether Jesus Christ would turn out to be the decisive fact for understanding the human situation in the world, or whether the current world-understandings would, in the end, place the things concerning Jesus Christ in *their* context. That is to say, would the current mythology determine the understanding of the things concerning Jesus Christ, or would the things concerning Jesus Christ be able to assert their fact-like properties sufficiently to make a decisive and definitive modification of the mythology? I have no doubt that it is the essential property of the things concerning Jesus that they do, under the inspiration of God, succeed in controlling every mythology in the interests of human openness, freedom and fulfilment. What I mean by this, it is the task of the second half of the lectures to demonstrate. Here and now I am concerned to outline the way in which the things concerning Jesus gave a new and decisive look to the current world understandings of the early centuries.

The existence and significance of Jesus Christ gave renewed grounds for the belief that men and the world fitted together. The Logos-language was a way of talking about the fitting-together of men and the world. It was, therefore, both natural and proper to use this Logos-language to express the discovered truth about Jesus. But the way in which the Logos-language was used to describe Jesus, and thus to describe his significance for the proper understanding of the world and of man's life in it, must be consistent with and, indeed, required by, the basic given shape of the things concerning

Jesus. The control for the use of the cosmic intuitions and under-standings which gave the original meanings to the Logos-language had to come from the original tradition which had made possible the recognition of Jesus as the Messiah, which had been vindicated by the fact that there was a Messiah because the Messiah was Jesus, and which had been re-defined by the actual shape of the life of this Jesus. Unless this control was maintained, there would be no given grounds in the world and in history for our attitude to the world and to history other than the fact that we have these attitudes. It would simply be a question of one mythology coming to terms with another mythology in order to produce a third which would simply last until fashions in thinking changed once again.

Christianity, however, did not allow the Greek fashion of thinking, which optimistically assumed the universe was rational, to be dis-placed by the Gnostic fashion of thinking which pessimistically assumed that men and the world did not fit together. The Gnostics insisted on, or assumed, a complete dualism between the truly spiritual and human on the one hand and the givenness of material things and of the events of history on the other. The Christian on the basis of Jesus Christ made what was essentially an optimistic asser-tion in a new way. He insisted that somehow the truly human and spiritual must be understood to be related positively and hopefully to the materiality of things and the happenings of history. One way of doing this in the thought-forms then existing was to insist that Jesus Christ was the Logos of the cosmos and thereby to define the Logos of the cosmos by Jesus Christ.

But here the current ways of thinking which existed independently of the things concerning Jesus Christ fought back, and that within the Christian Church, to produce the acute crisis of the fourth century which was known as Arianism. Even Greek optimism had not conceived that man and the cosmos fitted together in a way that took account of the material and bodily side of man, still less that took account of the serial events of history. It was the purely spiritual, rational, and mind side of man which was related to the underlying spiritual and rational pattern of the universe, and which was capable of ignoring the meaningless recurrence of the events of history and of penetrating the mere appearance of material things and so reaching the reality of true and absolute Being. God could never be thought of as in any way involved with the stuff of material things and the events of history, nor could value be found in or through such things. Thus, when Jesus Christ, who had been identified in his original context as the Son of God, because of his unique obedience to his unique rôle in relation to the bringing in of the Kingdom of God, was shown on the basis of this role to be also the Logos of the cosmos, a revulsion of feeling set in.

The original records about Jesus Christ made it clear that he was subject to human limitations and very much involved in the stuff both of materiality and of history. Arius and his followers who wished to retain the name of Christian (for there is something very attractive about Jesus Christ) while retaining also the assumptions of pagans (for there is something very attractive about thinking what everybody easily and currently finds thinkable) concluded that Jesus Christ could not be the true Son of God nor indeed the true Logos in the sense of the true pattern of the one, true, absolute and transcendent God. Rather, he could be the Son of God and the Logos of the cosmos only in the derived and watered-down sense that he had been created in a special and unique way in order to be responsible for all other creating, and capable of involvement in materiality and history.

Such a theory is pure mythology of the crudest sort which assumes that God, ultimate reality and absolute values cannot be related to the world or men, that is, to anything less than or other than himself, but that the gap can be bridged by an invented super-creature who is neither here nor there. As well as being nonsense in itself, such a mythology is straightforwardly contradictory of the Christian understanding of God and the world required by the things concerning Jesus. Jesus Christ makes it plain that history produces the key to the cosmos and that the pattern and power of the Kingdom of God is focused on a being who, however else he is to be understood, is certainly a man involved in materiality and history. Thus, however contradictory the notion of such an involvement of ultimate reality and absolute value in materiality and history might be to current ways of thinking, the things concerning Jesus demand that the notion should not only be thought, but also be asserted as true. And it was this Christian implication and assertion which Athanasius helped the Christian Church to make and to focus on the famous or notorious word *homoousios* which is translated in the Creed as 'of one substance'. Jesus Christ is 'of one substance with the Father', that is to say, he is truly Son of God and truly the Logos of the cosmos. He is truly representative of, and definitive of, the God who makes sense of history, truly representative of the pattern which fits together men and the universe. Conversely this means that whatever men have hitherto found thinkable they must now understand that God, however much he is to be thought of as the ultimately and the absolutely valuable, however much he is to be thought of as other than the events of history or the stuff of materiality, is also to be thought of as involved in, concerned with, and active through, things and happenings. Transcendence is no necessary bar to immanence, materiality is no necessary bar to spirituality, and change and process are no necessary bar to absoluteness and fulfilment. In fact, man and the universe fit together because of the involvement of God to that end.

But having reached this understanding of God and the world as required by the things concerning Jesus, the Christians were then faced with further acute problems. If Jesus Christ was rightly understood as the involvement of God in history and materiality for the sake of man, how could his person, his historical existence, be understood? This was the subject of the christological debates, the sometimes bitter discussion concerning the person of Jesus Christ, which culminated in 451 in the Definition of the Council of Chalcedon. In closing this lecture I must outline the structure of this Definition. The meaning of the Definition and the truth-claims which it makes on the basis of the things concerning Jesus are to be explored throughout the second half of the lectures.

The Definition stated that the existence who is Jesus Christ our Lord, and who is identical with the Jesus of Nazareth of the gospel records, is rightly and necessarily to be understood as truly and fully God, truly and fully man, and truly and fully one. The focusing formula of this is usually translated into English as 'one person in two natures'. Until we have had time to discuss this, both the terms 'person' and 'nature' as here used must be understood more or less as ciphers. 'Person' stands for 'one existent reality', in fact for the personal and historical individual designated Jesus of Nazareth. 'Nature' stands for all that is required to be truly God and all that is required to be truly a man. Thus the Definition asserts that the proper Christian understanding is that our Lord Jesus Christ who is Jesus of Nazareth is all that is required to be God and all that is required to be a man. It also goes on to state that all that is required to be God does not contradict, diminish or distort all that is required to be man, and all that is required to be man does not conflict with or lessen or alter all that is required to be God—and that further, the co-existence of all that is required to be God and of all that is required to be man does not mean any separation or division. There is and remains one Jesus Christ, perfect in Godhead, perfect in manhood, and perfect in unity. (One of the ways in which the Definition puts it is that 'the properties of either nature are preserved' and there is 'one and the same Lord Jesus Christ').

This is to say that to hold on to what the things concerning Jesus have shown to be true concerning the involvement of God in materiality and history for the sake of man, one must face a new and clearly articulated truth claim about the underlying structure of the relationship between God, man and the world. Briefly it is this. God is and remains all that is required to be God and this includes his absolute distinctness from everything else. God is in no sense the same thing as man or as anything that gets its existence from historicity and materiality. But in the purposes of God and by the power of God these two necessarily distinct ways of existing, of being God depending on himself and of being man depending on materiality and historicity, are drawn together into a perfection of unity which is wholly consistent with the essential requirements of each existence. We shall consider how this *could* be asserted when we explore in relation to certain trends in modern thought how something like this *can* be and *needs* to be asserted.

Meanwhile, we must rest on the first outline of the position that the structure of the definitive fact who is Jesus Christ came to be seen to be the *union* of the transcendent reality of God and the historico-material reality of man without the reduction of the one to the other. We shall have to see if this is meaningful by investigating its implications for our understanding of our human existence within the realities of the universe and of history. This investigation, I believe, will show that the things concerning Jesus which build up to the articulation of the Chalcedonian Definition lead us to understand that all theology may, as Feuerbach said, be understood as anthropology. But this is truly so only because all anthropology must be understood as theology.

V

The Exclusion of God

OUR CONCERN IS with persons. It can scarcely be otherwise. For even if we do not sufficiently know what personality is or how personalness should be defined, we are ourselves persons and cannot escape the concern which arises from being ourselves. Thus our concern is with persons even if the circumstances of our own living and the conditions of our own self-understanding lead us to treat this as a negative concern. That is to say, we may conclude that the proper policy to follow is one of detachment and withdrawal which leads to an escape from being a self and from concern with personality. But whether we consciously or unconsciously follow a policy of development of personalness or a policy of escape from personalness, as we are we cannot but be concerned with persons. The internal quality of this concern, and the external possibilities of this concern, combined with the external and internal threats to the concern, force us to see that our concern is also a question. What is it or could it be to be a person? Who am I? And what chance have I of either being myself or of escaping from myself?

Here we have what would seem to be a most subjective set of questions. Must I not decide for myself how I am to come to terms with what it is to be myself? But however unique may seem to be the self-conscious awareness of what it is to me to be myself, I have also to reckon with the fact that many aspects of me are wholly or largely continuous with that which is not me. Considered as a physical organism, I am wholly continuous with the stuff of the universe at large. *My* make-up is simply an example of the general make-up of human beings, and this is analyzable down through its various levels of organization, through cellular units, molecular units, atomic units and beyond. When one reaches this level of analysis, there is not only no difference between the units which eventually make up 'me' and those which make up 'you'; there is not even any difference between the units which make up human beings and any other organic matter. Indeed, at ultimate levels of analysis there is no difference between the units of organic and inorganic matter. In an analogous way, much, at any rate, of the physical, ethical, cultural and social features which make up the pattern which is 'I myself' is produced by, and continuous with, the larger patterns of which I am part, such as family, class, my particular society and so on. Thus I may have an intuition, which may well be supportable on a number of grounds, that I have a unique existence. It is, on the other hand, quite sufficiently clear that I have a general existence. Whatever else I may be, I am certainly simply one of the immense range of existents in the universe at large. If, therefore, I find myself facing the question 'Who am I?', I find myself facing the question of what data is available to assist me in answering the question. What is the status as data of my intuition of my uniqueness and of my caring for other persons? If I treat this sort of thing as data (and certainly it is part of the givenness of my own situation), how is it related as data to the data arrived at by forgetting my uniqueness and considering my general existence and by analyzing that into its various component parts or under its various appropriate headings? Is there, moreover, any data, anything given, which has a right to serve as definitive data, as that which is decisive for answering the question about my existence and for relating the various sorts of data to one another?

I have been arguing that the definitive data is the givenness of Jesus Christ. Or rather, I have been outlining the way in which that argument came into existence and the form which it took. I presume, certainly I hope, that in doing this I have made it clear that I am myself convinced that this is a true argument. But I hope also that I have made it clear, and shall continue to make it clear, that the argument, while it necessarily proceeds from conviction, is also an open one. This is to say, at least, that it can carry force only for those who enter into it in commitment and exploration, that it is an approach to the whole of life which cannot in this life be finally proved to be true, and that it is an argument, the direction of which is clear enough, but whose final bearing and whole fulfilment is not yet known to us. The significance of this openness of the argument for our understanding of the reality of man and of the truth of God will be considered at some length in the last two lectures. Here we are engaged in returning from our necessarily, but regrettably, brief excursion into the historical discovery and development of the force and shape of the Christian argument to our present concerns about the nature, place, scope and hope of man in the universe.

The Christian discovery on the basis of the givenness of Jesus Christ was that man and the universe hold together because of the involvement of God to that end. Thus materiality and history provide the stuff for the attainment of ultimate reality and the fulfilment of absolute value. The distinctive Christian understanding of man and the universe is that, to do justice to the realities involved therein, and to be experienced by man and through his life in the world, it is necessary to hold in distinction, and yet in union, that which is transcendent and wholly other to the universe and that which is immanent and wholly continuous with the universe. This understanding crystallized out into a doctrine of the person of Jesus Christ and has its symbol and safeguard in the fifth century Chalcedonian Definition. This is a confession of faith, an acknowledgement of what is found to be involved in responding to the givenness of Jesus Christ. Our Lord Jesus Christ is known as, and to be acknowledged as, one person in two natures. He who is the one personal existence who was historically named Jesus of Nazareth is perfect in Godhead and perfect in manhood, all that is involved in being God and all that is involved in being man. But the differences of the natures are in no way taken away by the perfection of the union and the unity. That is to say God remains God and man remains man and the absolutely fundamental difference between God in his transcendent independence and man in his dependent creatureliness is fully reaffirmed and maintained. God is God and man is man although the one Lord Jesus Christ is both—and yet one.

I shall attempt to show in the last two lectures that while this can, of course, be dismissed as unbelievable, it is by no means necessarily nonsense. I have tried in the preceding two lectures to set out the sort of grounds on which this claim came to be made. I am concerned now with the shape of what was claimed, with this twofoldness of distinction held to be in union. It is a shape of the utmost importance for our concern which I have just been recapitulating at the beginning of this lecture. It is maintained that the essential pattern of the man Jesus of Nazareth who is the Christ of God is the essential pattern of this God. The one Lord Jesus Christ exists in two natures and is all that is involved in being God and all that is involved in being man. That is to say that the name 'Jesus' not only designates the man but also designates him who is rightly thought of as being the Son of God who is 'of one substance with the Father'. The being who is Jesus Christ presents and represents the essential pattern and stuff or, if you prefer it, the true character and personality of the existence who is God. So Jesus Christ is the Logos of the cosmos. He is the presentation of that which gives the universe its shape and purpose, that indeed which ensures that it is a universe, i.e. a coherent whole. He is this because he is the embodiment and expression in materiality and history of the purpose and pattern of the God who works through materiality and history—who is Creator and Lord. Thus Jesus Christ is the expression in materiality and history of that which transcends and is independent of materiality and history. That transcendence and independence is not taken away by the involvement and identification. The properties of the Godhead are in no way diminished by the reality of the union.

On the other hand, the involvement and the union are wholly real. The properties of the manhood are in no way taken away by the union with the Godhead. Jesus is truly man, truly flesh, truly that which, biblically speaking, is created from the dust. The Bible is completely clear that man is in his physical make-up wholly continuous with the rest of the universe. Any privileged position which man enjoys or has the chance of enjoying does not proceed from his intrinsic make-up but from the possibilities which lie in his potential relationship with God. Analytically, he is a homogeneous part of the created universe. Thus Jesus Christ, because he is a man, is, like every other man, continuous as a physical organism with the whole of the rest of the universe. There is no more of an evolutionary break between the cooling of a spiral nebula and the man Jesus than there is in the case of any one of us. Between the cosmic dust and us there is no discontinuity. So Jesus Christ is all that is involved in being man including the possibility of analytical reduction to whatever are the units of the stuff of the universe.

But the Chalcedonian Definition is a symbol of the discovery and assertion that in the purposes of the transcendent and independent God, and by the power of this God, a union has been achieved between that evolutionary product of cosmic dust which is a human being and that transcendent and wholly other purposeful personalness who is God. Transcendent and independent personalness is at one with derived, dependent and evolved personality whose whole basis can be reduced to that impersonal materiality out of which it has developed and on which it depends. And the result is the personal union of God and man who is himself the person, Jesus Christ. In this there is discovered the personal fulfilment both of God and of man. We have the fulfilment of the personalness of God because God has achieved the expression of his purpose of love. This is the expression in conditions of materiality and history of an always perfect love so it is not a development of divine personalness. But to this we shall return in the last lecture. On the other hand we have the fulfilment of the personalness of man in the coming into existence of a perfection of relationship with God which is a personal and permanent union. But this we must consider in the seventh lecture. Meanwhile, we must be careful to note the shape of what is involved here. It is that God provides the fulfilment of his personal purposes for materiality and history by involving himself to the point where there is a personal union between transcendent personalness and derived personalness. This derived personalness is acknowledged as being wholly continuous with the impersonal stuff of the universe at large, but it is none the less asserted that such derived personalness can be lifted out of dependence on impersonal stuff, into a personal union with underived and transcendent personalness. Thus there is no denial of the immense difference between God and everything else nor of the fact that man's existence is rooted in the realm of 'everything else'. Man is clearly part of what we would call 'the universe known to science' and this is *not*

God nor continuous with God. But God unites the personal possibilities of this universe to himself in a personal union which does not destroy the distinction but achieves the personal purpose. Transcendent personalness and derived personalness are united by the immanence of the transcendent. Such is the pattern which the Chalcedonian Definition proclaims and defends. There is a union of two-foldness, of God and man, through the activity and presence of God. We do not have to choose between unique personalness and general impersonalness because God is concerned to produce and unite persons for himself out of the processes of materiality and history.

Such is the shape of the Chalcedonian Definition and its implications with regard to the questions which are of particular concern to us. Before one writes all this off as metaphysical speculation based on outmoded mythology, it is important to recall that the *structure* of this Definition was not evolved out of mere theorizing to fit in either with what men found thinkable or with what they wanted to find thinkable about themselves and the universe. This structure was evolved against the grain of the thought of the time. This thought was pessimistic about the possibilities both of materiality and of history, and strongly opposed to any idea of the involvement of God in the human and realistic way which is presupposed by the Christian definitions against the Arians and by the Definition of Chalcedon. It is a superficial mistake unsupported by a detailed study of the evidence to speak of the fourth and fifth century development of the doctrine of the Incarnation as if it were a Christianized version of a pagan and mythological theophany. The really impressive thing is that despite all the pressures upon Christians to think like that, for they were naturally men of their age as we are of ours, and despite the fact that many Christians did tend to think in terms of a God appearing as a man, the definitive pronouncements on the subject of the person of Jesus Christ steered clear of any such view and propounded a unique and very difficult doctrine. Indeed the understanding was so unique and so difficult to grasp in all its implications that, as we shall shortly see, the Church which had propounded it scarcely appreciated it and certainly often lost sight of many aspects of it.

I shall argue in the last two lectures that we are still only on the way to seeing further into its implications and applications and need in our turn to think very carefully about the understanding of God, man and the world which is demanded by this doctrine of the person of Jesus Christ. None the less it is sufficiently clear that despite all the natural pressures of the time and all the shortcomings of understanding and application, the Church of the time was led to evolve this unique statement of the *union* of God and man in and as Jesus Christ. Jesus Christ was not a theophany, that is he was not God or a God appearing as a man, a non-human being looking like and entering into the affairs of human beings. In the debates before the formulation of the Chalcedonian Definition and after it, much Christian writing and discussing came perilously close to this or actually did speak like this. But the Definition itself denies and rejects any such idea. Nor, on the other hand, is Jesus Christ to be understood simply as a man of such unique and heroic spiritual and moral stature that he is to be understood as having achieved or received God-like stature. Much modern thought in particular has felt obliged to reunderstand or misunderstand the Christian understanding of Jesus in this form. But this does not do justice to the understanding of Jesus as the Christ and Jesus Christ as Lord which formed the Church and which the Church felt bound to proclaim and defend. The discovery that Jesus was the Christ led to the discovery that he was the involvement of God and not just the attainment of man. Thus nothing but a two-fold structure understood as a personal union which had its historical expression in and as Jesus Christ was found adequate. This was necessary to hold together all the aspects of God's activity for man as it was known and understood in and through Jesus Christ. The Chalcedonian Definition is an outstanding and highly significant example of the creative and original power of the things concerning Jesus as they were experienced by the first disciples and renewed in the life-experience of the Christians who had in their turn to face the questions of the world and of themselves about the proper understanding of man's existence. The facts about Jesus required one to be clear that Jesus was unequivocally God, unequivocally man and obviously one, simply himself. Hence one must understand the world, and man in his existence in the world, on the basis of the distinct realities of God and of the derived universe and of the certainty of the union of the two in the personal purposes of God.

This unique and original understanding of the ultimate nature of things given through Jesus Christ meant that whatever the problems and difficulties which arose in the life of men nevertheless the universe was not a system hostile to or indifferent to the personal purposes which were the concern of God and of men. In the long run, although not immediately, this understanding of things cleared the way for modern science, as we shall shortly consider. But while the root possibilities of science lay dormant in the Christian approach to the universe which gradually became explicit in the first five centuries, the other most important side of our Western approach to the life of men in the world was already receiving a great deal of expansion and development in these early centuries. This, of course, was our concern for personalness and for the individual.

It was the historical Jesus Christ who presented to us the Logos of the cosmos. Thus men who shared the Christian faith in, and understanding of, Jesus Christ not only knew *that* men and the universe fitted together in and through the purpose of God, they also had some understanding of *how* this fitting together occurred. The 'how' was defined or at any rate pointed to by the actual character of the living and dying of the Jesus discovered to be the Christ and thus the Lord and so the Logos of the universe. We shall need to go into this more fully in the last two lectures. Here it is sufficient to note that while the fact that there was a Christ made it clear that there was unquestionably a God who saved men from being trapped in themselves and in the anti-human features of materiality and history, the actual nature of this Christ confirmed and re-defined the nature, activity and power of this God as being rightly understood primarily as love of a peculiar and distinctive kind. This love was the self-giving, identifying and involved love demonstrated by Jesus and commended by him through both example and commandment. It was so distinctive in its total self-identification with the loved that it was necessary to develop a little-used word, *agapē*, to refer to this love and so distinguish it from such types of love as those involved in ordinary friendship or ordinary sexual relationships which could be (although they need not be) self-centred.

Thus to know that Jesus Christ was the Logos of the cosmos and the Son of God was to know that the pattern and purpose at work in and throughout the universe was concerned with the fulfilment of each and every human-being in his or her own particularity as well as in his or her relationships. In fact the defining characteristic of every human being lies in his or her potential personal relationship to God in Jesus Christ rather than in any general or impersonal classification by status, class or any other category. Thus, while Christians have continued to fail to live up to this, it has always been a necessary implication of their response to the givenness of Jesus Christ that it should be clearly understood that in, and in relation to, ultimate reality every man and woman in his or her own particularity is of ultimate concern and of absolute worth. In the Christian view, that is to say in the way of understanding which is required by the reality of Jesus Christ, this value is rooted in the fact of God's unconditional loving concern, and ultimately to define or classify men in any other way is a mistake both of fact and of value.

Hence the Christian understanding of the true relationship between personal purposes and the processes of materiality and history makes it clear that there is, or at any rate, can be, always room for the development of the personalness of each individual. There is the possibility of freedom from the determinism of any classification or of any generalized situation which dissolves personalities into mere statistical units. This possibility is to be found in the activity of that infinitely resourceful love which is distinctively designated as *agapē*. No person need be defined or delimited by the impersonal and general features of his or her situation and existence.

But the proper understanding of the reality of Jesus Christ does not only make clear to us this freedom from the threatening determinism of the general through the possibilities of the universal scope of the love of God which liberates personalness for development and defines its infinite possibilities. There is a parallel implication that the facts of the universe are thrown open to the untrammelled investigation of science and technology. This implication arises because to discover that the Logos of the cosmos is that Jesus who is the Christ of the God who is the Lord of history is to know finally and decisively that all other divine elements in the universe have lost their rank and their power. Nothing other than that personal power who is presented in Jesus ultimately controls or underlies all that exists. You may continue to believe in demons, evil angels and even Satan, if you are conditioned to find this reasonable and not superstitious, but they are *not* 'world rulers', not built-in parts of the ordered and ordering power of the universe. Nor is it possible any longer to regard the planets or any other observable manifestation of a fixed order or regular motion in the universe as gods who control the order of the world and the life of man within the fixed pattern of their own inevitable revolutions. In fact the universe has become finally desacralized, emptied of any claim to divinity in its own right, and so free for the possibility of sanctification through personal activity. The stuff, patterns, processes and powers of the universe can now be known to be strictly neutral, neither beneficent nor malignant, and certainly not determined against men. The universe thus secularized is fully and freely open to the most rigorous probings that men can bring to bear, and the stuff and the processes of the universe lie neutrally available to be put to any end of which men can discover them to be patient. The whole of the universe is thus set free for the investigation of science and the development of technology. Because the universe is not divine, nothing bars man's free access to it. There is no numinous tabu or inhuman mystery keeping men at a distance. But, further, because it is created by the God and Father of Jesus Christ and sustained as a universe by the ordering power, the Logos, who is presented in and as Jesus Christ, the universe has to be treated authentically and seriously in its own right. It is an established and ordered given—true, a dependent given—but none the less given, and a given which proceeds from personal purposes and is open to personal purpose. Thus the universe has no divinity or personality of its own which can obtrude into or obfuscate the strict objectivity of the processes of true science, but it has its own authentic givenness which demands the strict objectivity of serious and open research and experiment and it is open to the manipulation of personal purposes.

Thus to discover that Jesus is the Christ, the Lord and the Logos of the cosmos is to discover that men are set free for the development of personalness and that the universe is set free as the material for science. The implication of the discovery that Jesus Christ is the defining datum in relation to all other data is that men have offered to them the possibilities of personalness, freedom and science. However, there is no case for, or point in, claiming that Christianity as a historical and cultural phenomenon is, as such, the 'cause' of modern science and technology. What I have been pointing out is that the things concerning Jesus do actually and intrinsically imply, demand and permit just that openness, neutrality and givenness of the stuff of the universe which is assumed in the activities of science and technology. None the less the *logical* connection between the implications of the things concerning Jesus and the required assumptions for the development of science and technology were certainly not mirrored in the *historical* relationships between organized Christianity and developing science and scientists. It is this variance between the truth as it is implied by the things concerning Jesus and the way things developed within the Christian Church in its attitude to science which we must now go on to consider.

The actual conditions of men's living in the fourth and fifth centuries of the Christian era and for many centuries beyond these were by no means favourable to the development of the whole range of potentialities which, we can now discern, were undoubtedly implied by the things concerning Jesus. Life remained, on the whole, 'nasty, brutish and short' and the Christian message of liberation for infinite development tended inevitably to concentrate on the aspect of the liberation of the individual personality for the infinite development of the relationship with God through the relationship of the individuals with God. Thus Christianity in the West tended to be centred more and more on the freeing of the individual from his burden of sin, while in the East the living heart of Christian spirituality was to be found in the pursuit of that ever-closer identification of the soul with God which led to 'deification', to the transfusion of the whole life of the believer with the very life of God. And the path to deification was by way of the *askēsis*, the discipline and training of withdrawal. Of course, such generalizations are gross over-simplifications. In the West from Augustine's

City of God onwards there was much concern with society, the state, and with innumerable problems of men's lives and the context of men's lives, while the East, as can be seen from iconography as well as from spirituality, always retained the vision of *cosmic* redemption, of Christ as the last Adam and head of the redeemed race of men and of the eventual penetration of the universe by the uncreated glory of God. None the less, in practice Christianity was not much concerned with the liberation and development of the natural powers in the universe—indeed there was no technique available to bring about such liberation.

These techniques, which are now so splendidly open to us in wide measure and which have every prospect of further vast increases in range, began to be produced as modern science developed from, say, the sixteenth century onwards, with its greatest acceleration in our time. But Christianity, having settled down into its mediaeval moulds, was largely unable to 'take' the strictly neutral and secular approach to everything in the universe (including eventually, man in so far as he is homogeneous with the rest of the universe), which is the essence of the scientific approach and which gives it its liberating and creative effect. Thus scientific developments were frequently seen, and indeed still are seen, as threats to the Christian religion. In this we have what is perhaps the most outstanding and the most disastrous example of the way in which the Christian religion—i.e. the alleged following of Jesus Christ as organized, practised and institutionalized—again and again gets off-centre from its true and only *raison d'être*—Jesus Christ himself. For Jesus Christ has neutralized and secularized the processes and stuff of the universe—albeit in relation to the purposes of God. But in so far as the Church pushed outside itself the Christian truth which lies in the scientific approach to the universe and to man in the universe, it is in no position to lord it over scientists who then proceeded to push out the other side of Christian truth about the universe and man— which is that all can properly be understood and handled only in relation to God. Scientists may have brought about the apparent exclusion of God, but if there is any point in allotting *blame* for this then we would probably do better to apportion it to the Church who attempted to confine the God and Father of Jesus Christ to the so-called sacred when Jesus Christ himself had already abolished the separation of sacred and secular *within* the universe. He had, of course, not destroyed the distinction between God and everything created, but that is something to which we shall return much later in the argument.

The most important effect of this hostility or, at best, lack of enthusiasm, in the relations between the Church and developing science is to be seen most clearly not in the contributors to the so-called war between religion and science but in those who continued to believe that Christianity and science somehow went together, for they affected the combination or co-existence in a disastrous and fundamentally un-Christian manner.

Descartes may be taken as symptomatic of the resultant false move, the more so as his influence contributed much to the development and ramification of this falsity. What Descartes did was to assume, and work on the basis of, a dichotomy between spirit and matter. Matter was the stuff of the universe which was the proper subject matter of the deterministic-type study of science. Spirit was, so to speak, the soul-stuff which was related to, and capable of, relationship with God.

The relationship of spirit to matter was a complete mystery. One just had to assume a parallelism between, say, the material movements open to the study of science which were involved in the muscular raising of an arm, and the spiritual activity which was the willing of the raising of the arm for the purpose of striking an angry blow. Men had to be thought of as physical organisms with a mysteriously parallel psychical life. And the distinction between the transcendent God and everything created became thought of in a way analogous to the dichotomy between spirit and matter within the universe. Spirit was God's realm and matter was the realm of science. The relationship between the two realms was a taken-for-granted parallelism which was also an insoluble mystery. For instance, how did the (spiritual) mind apprehend the reality of (material) objects? Locke, Hume, Berkeley and Kant all gave different and equally theoretical answers to this 'mystery'. Or again, how could the materially determined human organism be spiritually free? The relationship between the spiritual aspect of man and the material world had become an insoluble problem which had replaced the mystery of man's experience of the relationship between God and his creation. The effect of all this was to make one's belief in, commitment to, and practice of science one thing, and one's belief in God another.

God was the truly spiritual, who was not involved in or concerned with the universe as the subject of science. He could be known spiritually only. Thus if one were a Cartesian, one could know him inwardly by the clarity of the idea of God which reflection presented to one's mind. If one were a Kantian, one could know him only transcendentally when the wholly unique intuition of the moral imperative took one from the realm of the phenomenal to the wholly separate realm of freedom and immortality. Or if one followed the more deliberately theological solution of Schleiermacher, one apprehended God through the feeling of absolute dependence which was to be most carefully distinguished from knowledge, which gave one access to the scientific realm, and moral sense, which gave one access to the ethical. 'Religion', says Schleiermacher triumphantly, 'resigns all claim on science and morality'.

But in such a dichotomous situation it is clearly only a matter of time before we come to the obvious conclusion of Laplace concerning God. We have no need of *that* hypothesis. For as Kant himself pointed out against Descartes, clarity of idea implies nothing whatever about actual existence. And innumerable scientists in their pragmatism have outweighed Kant himself. The noumenal, the realm of freedom, immortality and God is, by Kant's own account, in no way known in the way in which scientific data is known. And the weight and effectiveness of scientific data is such that it is the scientific way of knowing which calls the tune as to what knowledge is. And in that case, where is the Kantian realm of the noumenal? And as to feelings of absolute dependence and judgements of value, are not feelings and judgements all our attitudes pure and simple? The fact that we have a godly attitude says nothing about the existence of God. Thus it turns out that theology is purely evaluative anthropology—the way in which we have hitherto expressed our understanding of the value of man. And Jesus Christ, if he is to be retained for a unique role at all, turns out to be the outstanding example of *our* understanding of the world and man. (For the Hegelian the realization of Spirit, for the existentialist the example of authentic existence and so on.)

When the realm of God was separated from the realm of science, it was supposed that the realm of God could be retained by making a corresponding dichotomy within man's approach to the universe and separating out the realm of spirit and the realm of matter. But the effect of this latter dichotomy in the history of thought was to reduce God to a hypothesis, a moral command or a feeling. Hence the way was open to discovering that we have no need of the hypothesis and that values and feelings are simply and decisively human. This prepared the way for the discovery that God is dead and Jesus, who strangely continues to exercise some compelling power for some, is then, if he is anything, the glory of man. We must leave it to the next lecture to face the evidence that if God is dead then man is dying.

VI

The Loss of Man

THE CHALCEDONIAN DEFINITION of the person of Jesus Christ stood for the belief and the assertion that the God who was transcendentally responsible for the existence of the universe and for the production of personal purpose out of the stuff of materiality and out of the events of history had become immanent in, and a part of, materiality and history, for the sake of his personal concern. This he had achieved by being the person whose name is Jesus, but not in such a way that the Creator was dissolved into a creature nor in such a way that the validity and authenticity of the creature was done away with or distorted in any way by the presence and power of the Creator. Thus it was asserted as literally true that materiality and history are capable of being led to produce an embodied and dependent personalness which is capable of union with transcendent and underived personalness. The homogeneous material universe is rightly understood as related to personal purposes because it finds its fulfilment in the natural organism man who is capable of receiving personal union with the transcendentally personal God.

So man with his personal and spiritual potentialities is not to be set over against the impersonal, indifferent and material universe of which he is none the less also mysteriously and seemingly tragically a part. Rather, a man is a wholly natural part of the universe which proceeds from, and is being moved towards, personal purposes. In man, the personal possibilities of the universe emerge and are brought to fulfilment by being brought into union with the personalness of the God from and for whose personal purposes the universe exists. Thus there is no dichotomy in man or between man in some particular aspect of his being and the rest of the universe. Man is a homogeneous, although not yet fully developed, whole and the particular pattern and structure which constitutes man is itself a pattern and structure within and homogeneous with the pattern and structure of the whole universe. The *distinction* with which the Chalcedonian Definition is concerned is the same distinction with which the whole tradition of biblical theism is concerned. This is the distinction between the totality of the universe, the sum-total of everything that is 'created', and the God and Creator who is transcendent to and other than the universe.

But this distinction is not a *dichotomy*. God and the universe are not kept apart in some inexplicable parallelism wherein the material events of the universe have some shadowy set of spiritual and divine parallels. God and the universe in their respective distinctivenesses, in their two distinct 'natures', are closely involved, although not confused. This involvement is throughout the product of the untrammelled will and purpose of God. The transcendence of God remains untouched. He is in no way dependent for his being God on either the existence or the events of the universe. But the universe depends for its existence and its fulfilment entirely on God. This is the first involvement. There is no dichotomy between God and the universe, because God is in the closest possible touch with the universe as its originating, continuing and consummating cause. The second involvement lies in the presence and activity of God in the processes of materiality and in the events of history to produce a development whereby there shall emerge personal beings capable of a personal knowledge of and response to himself. This involvement includes also the presence and activity whereby these personal beings do actually become aware of the personal reality who is God. The first involvement corresponds very broadly to that which would come in traditional theology under the heading of Creation, while the second comes, again very broadly, under the heading of Revelation. The third involvement is the personal presence of God in and as Jesus Christ. This is fully personal in the sense that God is present in his personalness, that Jesus is a fully human person, and in the sense that the union of God and man is the person, Jesus Christ. Thus Creation, Revelation and Incarnation all speak of the involvement of the distinctive God in the universe for the fulfilment of his personal purposes. These purposes are so personal that the absolute distinction whereby God in his wholly unique and independent Godness transcends everything else is itself transcended or fulfilled in a perfect union with the personalness that has emerged from the dependent and derived 'everything else' which is so distinct from God.

All this implies that any Christianity which is continuous with the reality and revelation of Jesus Christ must be deeply and fully conerned with the widest possible exploration of every feature of the universe and of every opportunity and possibility which it offers to the personal activities and concerns of men. But, as we know only too well and as I discussed briefly in the last lecture, the exploration of the universe and development of its practical possibilities through science and technology have very largely been seen as hostile to Christianity both from within and from without the Christian faith. There can be no doubt whatever that this is a mistake and it is a mistake which has done far more than threaten the continuing existence of the Church. It has led to a threat to the continuing existence of the humanity of man.

I have used a reference to Descartes to draw attention to the dichotomy which has characterized modern man's understanding of himself and of his existence in the world in relation both to the development of science and technology and in relation to his knowledge and understanding of God. It is most important to take full note that it is 'dichotomy' which is the correct word here and not the word 'distinction'. For there is no question of the involvement of two existences or natures which are distinct but which have a purposeful and personal relationship leading to a union. There is no involvement of mind and matter. There is only the theoretically assumed mystery which is really only a mystifying and insoluble puzzle of how two totally and necessarily (by definition) distinct types of existence none the less co-exist in parallel and perform a series of shadow dances.

This is a pretty desperate expedient to try and hold on to the materialistic and deterministic side of things on the one hand, and to the free, human and spiritual on the other. But thinkers like Descartes and Kant and, indeed, their successors down to our own time, were in a pretty desperate situation. It seemed clear to them that science and technology advance by methods that are necessarily neutral, impersonal and deterministic. It was also clear that if such methods extend exhaustively to everything that can in any sense be said to exist then the essentially human, spiritual and lively aspects of our existence as free or potentially free persons are done away with. Further, there was no assistance or illumination from theology or from officially Christian thinking to baptize this situation as a whole into an understanding which could see the neutral and deterministic material of science as clearly within a transcendent personal purpose. Rather, the Church fell back on its own sacred realm as over against the powerful growing secular and scientific realm by which it was increasingly threatened. Since many of the thinkers who knew the power and authenticity of science wanted to go on believing in God, and since all of them wanted to go on believing in man, they were forced back on an essentially atheistic way of conceiving the relationship between the material, impersonal and deterministic aspect and the spiritual, personal and human aspect of existence as known to men. Further, this relationship is not only essentially atheistic, it is not even in reality a relationship.

To preserve the full force of both aspects of existence, a dichotomy was assumed between them. This would keep science free from the confusion of the personal, and the personal free from the stranglehold of determinism, while God was left to go on being God as long as men had a clear idea of him. But what kept the dichotomy together, and *a fortiori*, what kept God attached to any part of it? The last part of this question is not mere rhetoric, because the original perpetrators of, and thinkers about, the dichotomy, such as Descartes and Berkeley, assumed that it was God who kept the dichotomy together. The situation of existence was in this dichotomous form because God had so arranged it and so sustained it. But God does not long survive when his status becomes that of a hypothesis which needs no explanation in order to enable men to hold a hypothesis which does. (One might be inclined to assume that if God were godly he would not care to survive under such circumstances!) Even Kant's attempt to, so to speak, skewer together the two sides of the dichotomy, now known as the phenomenal and

the noumenal, by the self-evident intuition of the categorical imperative, and then to continue God in the rôle of guarantor that this
Kantian intuition was in fact an intuition of reality, did not do much
to prolong the life of the God-hypothesis. As the transcendent other
had been in effect excluded from any purposeful participation in the
affairs of materiality and history which was where the effective
knowledge and the effective experience of men lay, God was in fact
dying, although one has to wait for Nietzsche definitely to proclaim
the triumphant and the tragic fact of his death.

But with God out of the way, what then becomes of the dichotomy? It is left in its nakedness, to be seen as not even a relationship.
It is possible to make sense of, and go on believing in, a relationship
of personal purpose which exists between two distinct realities or
natures of which at least one is personal and purposeful. Thus, if
one has grounds for believing in a transcendent and personal God,
then it is perfectly possible to make sense of the notion of his having
a relationship of purpose and activity with anything completely distinct from him, with inert and impersonal matter as well as with
active and personal creatures. But it is not possible to make sense of a
relationship between what are held to be two distinct existences or
natures like mind and matter and, indeed, no one ever has. For mind
and matter are, *ex hypothesi*, two dichotomous aspects of, or existences within, the total existence of the universe which includes man
who, of course, shares in this dichotomy. But as far as our observations and experience go, neither 'mind' nor 'matter' are personal and
purposeful existences. The personal and purposeful existence known
to us is man who, already, on the theory, *consists* of the dichotomy.
Thus there is nothing to relate or hold together the dichotomy
which was in any case set up precisely because of the difficulties,
dangers and quite probable impossibility of the relationship. Man
has thus become an insoluble problem to himself. He has, indeed, an
impossible picture of himself.

Hegel attempted to solve the problem by promoting mind in the
mysterious form of *Geist*, or Spirit, to a purposeful although not a
personal and, in the traditional sense, not a transcendent reality. But
it is clear that Hegelianism is purely theoretical thinking designed to
answer problems which the history of thought has simply generated

for itself, and that it never comes down to dealing with actual historicity or materiality. Hegel and his followers thought that this was precisely the strength of his sytem. Pressure of space and time forces me to assume that you will agree with me that this flight from the actual realm of particular materiality and historicity into the doubtfully existent realm of the general and so called 'spiritual' is a form of escapism which has already given up hope of any realistic solution to the problem that man is to himself. There is a further fact which makes it decisively clear that Hegelianism is nothing but mythology, i.e. a theory which tells a tale about man and the nature of his existence in the world without any sufficient anchorage in the actual stuff of the world and of history. This is that Hegelianism can be simply stood on its head to produce Marxism, wherein the rôle of the purposeful but immanent and impersonal *Geist*, or spirit, is taken over by the apparently purposeful but most certainly impersonal dialectic of the *material* process.

In fact Hegelianism and Marxism show that the dichotomy of spirit and matter cannot be held. Either spirit or matter has to be promoted to the rôle of God, although the transcendent, personal God of the Bible is assumed to be unthinkable and therefore dead, and so this rôle has to be played by an immanent and impersonal force for whose existence there is, and can be, no sufficient evidence and which, indeed, would never have been thought of if it had not seemed necessary to find a thinkable substitute for the God of the Bible. But you cannot think up substitutes for God. If he is dead then he is dead. And with his death there is the decisive collapse of all mythologies which cling outmodedly to the view that materiality and historicity have a purposeful pattern which can be perceived by those who receive through secular prophets such as Hegel or Marx the clue to the inner although impersonal 'Logos' of the historical process. Purpose and pattern are a feature of personalness. Since there is no transcendent personalness, there is no overall purpose or pattern. There is not even open to us the freedom of the acceptance of necessity in becoming a conscious part of the dialectical process. For it is simply a myth of the human imagination that there is such a process. As far as our observation goes there is no process—only processes.

Marxism may fight an old-fashioned rearguard action, and certainly in its political effects it remains a force to be reckoned with—but not as a philosophy purveying truth about the world and about man's existence in the world. With the death of God it is clear that there is no Logos of the cosmos; that indeed, as Bertrand Russell has pointed out, we are not really entitled to use an expression like 'cosmos' or 'universe', with its implication that we are talking about a structured whole. What we face in arriving at our own self-understanding is the recognition of the reality of fragmentation. There is no sense to be made of anything, other than the sense which we can each of us make for ourselves. We are left with the problem of what is the relationship of that in us which wishes to make sense to the senselessness of everything else, including the rest of ourselves, but we know that this is both a problem and a senseless one. We are thus finally and definitely clear that we are an insoluble problem to ourselves.

There appear to be current two significant reactions to this existential situation of which the second has two distinctive forms. The first is to turn to various forms of Oriental monism or simply to various techniques of escape, yoga and the like, which can be detached from their attendant and consequent philosophy and be used very like drugs. We are an insoluble problem to ourselves and therefore we must practice techniques which enable us to cease to be aware of ourselves or even follow out a philosophy and practice which will ultimately set us free from being selves at all. Clearly this is, in the most literal sense, the absolute contradiction of that direction and activity of the self which has produced science and technology. The thinking, analyzing, organizing and practising self and all its achievements of knowledge about the universe and consequent power to better so many of the aspects of man's life in the universe has got to be eschewed and got rid of. We are to return to the oblivion of the womb, of not being a self, and to turn our backs decisively on all the achievements, possibilities and responsibilities of human living in a universe patient of scientific and technological manipulation. Such a personal choice, to deny and reject the opportunities and responsibilities of being a person, is clearly an acknowledgement of the total bankruptcy of man. The point of being human is to cease to be human. But to say that man is totally bankrupt is to choose to deny that the human achievements of science and technology are to count as achievements at all. But this is to make an arbitrary choice as to what counts as determining evidence about the human predicament on the basis of an already arrived at pessimism about the truth of the human predicament. There is, and can be, no evidence which compels the conclusion that all human thinking, achievements and possibilities are nothing but valueless illusions. Any philosophy and practice which alleges this must proceed from the decision that it is not humanly possible to cope with being human, so that what must be repudiated is humanness, and it must then read the evidence of the human condition in that light.

The fact that men are turning to such pessimistic and personality-denying practices and philosophies at a time when scientific and technological possibilities have reached an unprecedented level is one important symptom of the way in which the opposing, or at any rate the separating, of the realm of the scientific and material, and the realm of personal and spiritual, produces a situation in which the personal is repudiated and so the scientific becomes wholly futile. This is doubtless in the logic of the situation in which we have forced ourselves to the non-sense that we are insoluble and meaningless problems to ourselves, but in logic a false proposition can imply any conclusion whatever. Here we have one piece of non-sense producing or at any rate supporting another piece of non-sense.

The other symptomatic and rather commoner reaction to the awareness that the human situation exists in the face of fragmentation is the various forms of existentialism. These would seem to fall into two main types in which the predominant reaction to the realized nonsensicality of the human situation is either nausea in the face of the Absurd or courage in the face of despair. Nausea can lead to complete cynicism, hectic sensuality and meaningless triviality. This response is reflected in not a few plays and novels. Here it is clear enough that man is dead although he is not yet quite able to lie down. With courage in the face of despair, humanness is somehow maintained until the evident sentence of death is finally executed. But the protest has no final point. The sense which we can make for ourselves and the values which we can create for ourselves scarcely seem to burn brightly enough to illuminate humanity more than flicker-ingly. The main characteristic of the whole philosophy and approach is one of protest. But it is a negative protest against the whole human condition, not a positive protest against anti-humane features in that condition which are to be striven against for the sake of a deeper humanness. Man complains bitterly against his condition, but there is no-one to complain to and nothing to be gained by complaining.

Once again we have a complete contrast with the other side of the life of modern man, with the spirit of science and of technology. Here one does not complain. One diagnoses problems and works out how to programme solutions. There would thus seem to be a good deal of plausibility in the view that the Cartesian dichotomy has either itself led, or is symptomatic of a more general approach to the life of the world which has led, to a real and very destructive split in man's understanding of and hopes for himself. When operating on the scientific and material side he is optimistic and purposeful. When reflecting on the human and spiritual side he is pessimistic and hopeless, so much so that he is prepared in one way or another to write off the achievements of his scientific side and his own personal-ness with them.

But surely this is absurd—and straightforwardly so, not in any technical existentialist sense? (We may note in passing that this might be true but that logic does not prevent men practising absurdity if they have strong enough existential reasons for doing so.) After all, the achievements of men on what I have called the 'scientific side' are achievements of what must be called the human and spiritual side of man, if we are going to contrast material and spiritual in any way. Scientific optimism is as much the product of humanness as is existential despair. Is there not, therefore, a simple solution to the situation in which we find that we are insoluble problems to ourselves? Let us eschew existential problems and, *a fortiori*, the escapism of monistic withdrawal, and concentrate on the pursuit and practice of science and technology.

Now let us assume that this total putting on one side of existential and undermining questions is possible. (I do not for a moment believe that it is, has been or ever will be, but so many people who pride themselves on being scientific are so insistent on ignoring a whole range of the plainly observable features of human living for the sake of what they persist in calling scientific and empirical theories, that I am prepared to make the assumption for the sake of the argument.) We do not then ask existential questions, we concentrate on the pursuit of science and technology in order to avoid the pessimism so destructive of humanness and personality which we have been considering. What *then* happens to humanness and personalness? They are clearly threatened with even more certain extinction. For science and technology have, as such, no means of recognizing or reckoning with humanness and personalness. These reside in the particularity of individuals, however much they are built up by and from the individual's roots in both his physical and his social and human environment. But the impersonal, neutral and necessarily generalizing techniques of science and technology cannot possibly recognize individuals, still less personal individuals constituted as such by their own unique particularity and personalness. Social and human engineering and social and human science, in the sense that human individuals and human society are the *objects* of science and engineering, come very close to being contradictions in terms unless there is an awareness of the existential dimension of human personalness, which then prevents them from being purely scientific and technological. Existentialism may recognize that man in his humanness is dying, but science, if it indulges in unscientific optimism about its total capacity to deal with the problems of man, might much more easily kill off man's humanness without even noticing it.

I think it is quite sufficiently clear that man's humanness and personalness is threatened with death, and that not only in the sense that every individual human person must die. The whole of what has hitherto been glimpsed as being involved in a lively humanness and in a purposeful and particular personalness is threatened on the one hand by the enervating and consciously pointless complaining of a pessimistic existentialism, and on the other by an over-optimistic scientism. This latter supposes that science and technology can solve all human ills by statistical and generalizing methods which of necessity dissolve the particular qualities of humanness into the general qualities of materiality. Many men have lost their nerve to be human, while others have too much nerve on a front which is too narrow to have room for all that is involved in being human.

Must we then fall back on the position that human personalness is indeed always under threat, that it has no ultimate place in the scheme of things (which is in any case not a scheme) and that we must summon up what courage we can in the face of absurdity and despair to keep alive what personalness we may to whatever degree we may? And shall we find enough resources to do this in the face of all the changes and chances of humanity on the one hand and in the face of the all-conquering prestige of science on the other? Moreover, why try?

Here we might consider two things, one in the form of a further question, the other a statement. The question is, 'Why should science, which is the product of human-beings, threaten humanness?'. The statement is that Jesus Christ has made it clear that human personalness is a focus of reality which is at all costs to be maintained and developed. Let us proceed from the statement and return to the question.

When we are considering the Cartesian dichotomy, the Kantian categorical imperative, the Hegelian doctrine of Spirit, the Marxist view of dialectical materialism, Oriental forms of monism, or existential pessimism, we are considering theories which men have formulated about the total nature of things. This is as true of existentialism as of any other philosophy. These theories are formed because men choose particular features that they are aware of in the world and in their own existence as being of decisive significance for their understanding of the totality of existence. On the basis of this choice they erect their structure which is supposed to embrace the whole of existence, to give one one's complete and exhaustive picture. Thus all these philosophies, or rather all the philosophies which contain the features I have referred to, are exercises in metaphysical mythology or mythological metaphysics. They purport to give decisively true pictures of reality. In fact they are tales which men have chosen to tell with more or less reason, and with a greater or lesser degree of articulation, about the way they think reality should be apprehended and responded to.

Science can be turned into such a metaphysical mythology as

well. This happens when it is claimed that reality in the sense of all that exists and all that counts as existing in the long run is co-extensive with that which is or which can be investigated by science. When this happens, when for instance a biologist authoritatively assures us that man is essentially and definitively a biological organism, or a psychologist decisively claims that personality is really a matter of psycho-dynamics, then we have passed from science properly so called to metaphysical mythology. There is no absolutely decisive evidence, certainly no strictly scientific evidence, for seeing man or the universe as wholly within the framework of any particular science or of all the sciences. The person who demands or recommends that we should do so is simply registering the choice which he has made. He has decided to take scientific evidence as *the* decisive clue in the understanding of man and the world and to build his complete picture accordingly. It should perhaps be scarcely necessary to reiterate that this is not a scientific procedure. Total frameworks are not the products of scientific investigation but of human choice and imagination, including the total framework which consists in maintaining that there is no such thing, but only meaningless fragments.

Any framework, any metaphysical theory which has proved influential, has done so because it was not entirely arbitrary, or simply *mere* imagination and choice. The choice of the basis was clearly influenced by recognizable features in men's then current life and understanding, and the imagination which erected the structure was clearly guided by insights related to the same things. Thus powerfully influential metaphysical theories are not arbitrary. But however powerful and plausible they are, they are never final or bound to give the truth about things. Thus we need never be tied to any theory or philosophy save by our own choice.

We may choose to see ourselves and the world in some particular framework. We may say that we refuse to do anything of the kind and thus either be unaware that we are conforming to the prevalent spirit of the age or else, and much more rarely, be setting out to practice the impossible and be a consistent nihilist. Or we may choose Jesus Christ as our decisive point of reference and our defence against being shut up in any necessarily partial and inevitably misleading theory whatever. For Jesus Christ has the advantage over every theory that he has happened and was not just thought up. Much has been thought about him and Christians have again and again tried to destroy him by shutting him up in theories. But as I have tried to show in the first half of these lectures, I would claim that the essential insights which Jesus Christ makes available to us are derived from his happenedness and givenness and that it is he and the facts about him which control the truly Christian understanding of things. And as I shall try to show in the last two lectures, this understanding is not and never can be a theory which provides a frame which embraces everything. Rather it is, and must always be, open to new and hitherto unknown possibilities. In this I am convinced that true Christianity is precisely the same as true science. Both are required to be totally open to whatever is authentically given in each situation. This is no mere coincidence. For it is Jesus Christ who definitively makes it clear that the universe is truly open to truly scientific investigation.

With regard to our particular dilemma about why or how to go on being concerned with human personalness, I would simply say at this stage that my answer is that the happenedness of Jesus decisively reinforces the intuition which I discussed at length in the first lecture that our concern is with persons and that this concern can be resourcefully pursued. This is the main subject of the next lecture. With regard to the question why science, which is the product of human beings, should threaten humanness, I would now answer that this is so because with the exclusion of God, which is at least as much the fault of the Church as of the scientist, men lost the possibility of uniting the basically and originally impersonal and material resources of the universe with the personal purposes which *under God* became the decisive and distinctive concern of men. Thus the personal union of Chalcedon degenerates into the impersonal dichotomy of Descartes, and man becomes an insoluble problem to himself. As a result man either loses his wholeness by seeking to find his humanity in a desperate defiance quite apart from, and contrary to, science, as in existentialism, or loses his human personalness by succumbing to the generality and impersonality of science.

Thus at present we find man concentrated on his existential predicament. The result seems to be to bring him near to despairing of his humanness. As I pointed out, while European thought was on the way to this conclusion Feuerbach remarked that all theology was really anthropology. I propose that we should take up this very significant remark and see what becomes of the existential predicament of man if, and with the help of Jesus Christ, we see whether we may reconsider all anthropology as theology. Certainly the reduction of theology to anthropology was a prelude to reducing anthropology to absurdity. If we have grounds for re-understanding anthropology as theology, we may yet have hope that we can be rescued from the Absurd.

VII

Real Man

MAN IS NOT absurd. It would be nearer the truth to say that he is
divine. But if he is substituted for God, or if he denies God, then
he is nothing. Theology can be plausibly reduced to anthropology
because in reality man is in the image of God and depends for the
fulfilment of his humanness on the transcendent and personal reality
of God. As the image of God, man is truly human. Once, however,
man effectively rejects the idea that he is in the image of God and
decides that God is simply the shadow of man, then his essential
humanness is at the mercy of the massive impersonality and indifference of a godless and, *ipso facto*, inhuman universe. This absurd
situation arises because of the refusal or failure to understand that all
anthropology is inevitably theology. Man to be man requires God,
because God is the cause as he is the end of the emergence of man.

But what grounds have we for maintaining that anthropology is
ultimately and inevitably theology? Why is my foregoing paragraph
not just one more piece of metaphysical mythology whereby I
choose to defend myself from the absurdity of man by sheltering
behind the fantasy of God? The grounds for maintaining the
inevitable extension of anthropology into theology are two-fold.

Firstly, we have seen how the death of God strikes a mortal blow
at the humanness and personalness of man. But can we really and
reasonably lose faith in human personalness? It may be urged that
the apprehension of personalness and of the uniqueness of the
dimension of the person which I was particularly concerned to point
to in my first lecture is simply a set of epiphenomenal feelings which
happen to have arisen among a certain group of organisms which

happen to have been thrown up with this characteristic reaction-pattern. Thus it could be argued that the apprehension of personalness is no more significant of what reality is like in the end than, say, the fact that, as far as can be ascertained, most normal people react to a certain wavelength of light by seeing a colour called 'blue'. We happen to 'see a colour we call blue', whatever that means, and we happen 'to react to personalness', whatever *that* means. Or perhaps the situation would be even better characterized by pointing out that some people find blue a wonderful colour, others loathe it, and some are colour-blind. Why should we suppose that the apprehension of personalness is decisively different from this sort of thing?

There are at least three reasons, even at this level of the argument, for maintaining that the apprehension of personalness is decisively different from a reaction consisting in a set of epiphenomenal feelings. The first one is intuitive; I have already dwelt on it at some length and I must refer you back to it. You must take a long, hard and honest look at what is involved for you in being a person in relation to persons and see if you can reasonably and consistently commit yourself to the view that what is involved here is nothing but a reaction like excitement at red or boredom at green. The second reason for seeing more in the apprehension of personalness than mere feelings is what I would refer to as the observable mystery of persons. By this I mean the logical and practical impossibility of fitting human beings as persons into any single framework. This I have touched on in the first lecture, and said a good deal about in lectures V and VI. There is a clearly observable way in which human beings can and do transcend their environments and are recognizably different in their behaviour and their effects from non-human features of that environment. This is, of course, by no means always the case, but the cases where human personalness is recognizable are quite sufficient to give strong support to the view that in apprehending personalness we are becoming aware of a distinctive feature in things and not just having a feeling. Men are homogeneous with the rest of material creation, but it is an observable and objective fact that as human and personal they demand to be treated differently.

We may reasonably hold, therefore, that in observing personalness we are observing an objective and significant feature of things as they are, the more so when we take into account our third consideration, which is that of the moral and practical effects of distinctively human living. The personal qualities of human beings, especially of notable human beings at their most personal and individual, have made their mark on what can be done with, and what can be done within, the possibilities of materiality and history. The achievements of art, of technology and of science are indisputable, even if their evaluation can be a matter of debate. Thus we have very strong grounds for holding that in apprehending personalness we are apprehending some real feature in the emerging nature of things which is of particular significance. Faith in human personalness, therefore, is a very reasonable faith which has considerable claim to inform, if not direct, our reasoning.

We have, in fact, reasonable grounds for believing that anthropology ought not to be reducible to absurdity. Since this is so and since also we have seen that the elimination of theology from anthropology was related to and relatable to the reduction of anthropology to absurdity, we may at least entertain the idea that in fact anthropology does imply and involve theology. We have very strong, even if not decisive, grounds for retaining our faith in man. It may very well be, therefore, that we have equally strong grounds for hoping that we ought to retain our faith in God. Man is not dead. This may well be because God is not dead either.

It is important to be quite clear that this is not a 'God of the gaps' argument. That is to say, we are not suggesting faith in the liveliness of God in order to fill a gap which is said to be visible in the liveliness of man. The argument does not arise from finding a weakness in the situation of man which is then exploited into a gap into which God may be fitted as a cosmic anodyne and an anthropological placebo. The argument arises from the strength of the case for continuing to have faith in the liveliness of man. Man is not dead. Is there not something of the divine in his liveliness?

I would certainly claim that a careful inspection of, and reflection on, the most characteristically human aspects of the human situation provide much that can legitimately be taken as evidence of the divineness of man. This divineness is derived. Moreover, it is a divineness which is not only derived but also largely potential only,

for it is the divineness of a creature who is emerging out of materiality and history as a personal pattern capable of forming relationships
which are ultimately fulfillable in a relationship of union with the
uncreated and transcendent divinity of the true God himself. The
simplest way of referring to this quality of incipient and potential
divineness which is characteristic of that which is most human in
man, is to make use of the biblical notion that man is in the image of
God. He has built into the emerging pattern which is characteristically human a reflection of the freedom, transcendence and creati-
vity which is to be glimpsed in the divine personalness of God. Thus
I would summarize the first main argument for maintaining the
inevitable extension of anthropology into theology as lying in the
evidence of the liveliness of man despite the threat of absurdity
with which the alleged death of God has faced him. We may
reasonably continue to have faith in man, and this demands that
we re-examine the position with regard to faith in God. I have
interpolated into that argument an anticipatory comment of my
own which is that it is in fact in the liveliness of man that we see
evidences of that derived divineness which characterizes the reality
of man and which is best referred to by understanding man as being
in the image of God. He reflects divine qualities and is heading for
union with the divine personalness who is God.

But this particular comment of mine is intruding into the argument concerning the first ground for maintaining that anthropology
is inescapably theology something that is properly an extension of
the second ground. It may be reasonable to hold on to faith in man,
and some may even admit that it is reasonable to go on from faith in
man to reconsidering faith in God. But there is nothing absolutely
compelling about this reasoning, and some will certainly hold that it
is not really reasonable at all. I believe I have alleged reasonable
grounds for claiming human personalness as an objective feature of
reality as we know it, and for the claim that this feature of reality
deserves to be taken as a significant clue to an authentic and valid
approach to reality as a whole. But, as we have had occasion to
observe at various points throughout the lectures, men have been
confronted, and we are today confronted, with counter-claims about
the proper understanding of reality and our existence which some

hold to be equally reasonable and others hold to overwhelm all reason. We have, therefore, to be clear that the second ground for holding that anthropology is inevitably theology is not a set of reasons, but the givenness of a personal happening, that is to say the givenness of Jesus Christ.

Jesus was a particular man who lived out a particular pattern of life under particular circumstances. He happened. Through the happenings which focused on his personal particularity, he was recognized as the Christ of God, and from this it was seen that the shape of his happenedness presented in a form embodied in materiality and history the shape of the Logos of the cosmos. This recognition of Jesus as the Christ and of Jesus Christ as Lord and Logos is, of course, the recognition of faith. I have tried to indicate the type of grounds on which the Christian believer is entitled and, indeed obliged, to assert both to himself and to all believers or unbelievers that the recognition of faith is recognition and not composition. The shape of the happenedness of Jesus is an historical given which does set forth the shape of the Kingdom of God and therefore the shape of the personal pattern and purpose which is at work behind, in and beyond the patterns and processes of materiality and history. This is not a theory, but the faithful perception through experience and experiment wholly involved in things and events, of the pattern of the purposes of the God who transcends materiality and history. The decisive ground for being clear that anthropology implies theology is that the shape of the happenedness of the life of the man Jesus is wholly orientated towards God, and the significance of the life of the man Jesus is discovered to be the pattern of the purposes of God. The facts of the liveliness of man legitimately raise the question of the continuing livingness of God. The shape of the givenness of Jesus Christ answers the question both as to the reality of the livingness of God and as to the nature of the liveliness of man. For the rest of this lecture we must concentrate on Jesus Christ as the definition, demonstration and declaration of the reality of man, leaving to the last lecture some consideration of the witness of Jesus Christ to the truth about God.

Since Jesus Christ was a particular man who lived his own distinctive life his happenedness had its own particular shape. The discovery that Jesus was the Christ meant that this distinctive, particular shape of his life became definitive for the understanding of the realities of man's life and of the realities of God's dealings with men. This becomes immediately and importantly obvious at the very first stages of the life of Christianity by the way in which the shape of the life of Jesus demands, and indeed constitutes, a re-definition of the notion of 'Messiah'.

The fact that Jesus is the Messiah, the Christ, decisively de-mythologizes and universalizes the biblical and Jewish understanding of God, the pattern of his purposes and the methods of his activity. The build-up to the recognition of Jesus as the Christ I have already discussed, and I have given some indication of the way in which the notion of the Christ is related to that of the Kingdom of God and of how that notion was developed out of the experience of those people who became the Jews and was used by them as an expression of their faith in the consistency of the character and activity of the God they had come to know. Naturally, the whole set of ideas which included the picture of the Kingdom of God and the expectation of the Christ was imprecise, had at some points conflicting features, and contained a number of mythological elements. That is to say, a more or less consistent story was told about God and his dealings with men based on selected incidents and experiences in the past, which then passed over into a story which predicted the future of God's dealings with men.

With the discovery that Jesus is the Christ this story is discovered to come true in a twofold sense. Firstly, the story is vindicated as having its truth value rooted in the realities of materiality and history as known to men, out of which men have developed as men and in which men live as men and must strive to be human. I have already discussed this truth-establishing aspect of the discovery that Jesus is the Christ. For our present purposes it is the second side of the coming true of the story in Jesus as the Christ which is important. We now know on the basis of event and experience what is the true way of telling the story. Jesus who is the Christ is the way God acts. Jesus Christ is the visible embodiment of the pattern and powers of the Kingdom. If you want to know what you really ought to mean and what you are justified in meaning by telling a story about the love of God for men and the eventual hope of men in God, then you must consider the pattern of the living and dying of Jesus. He is not mythological, whatever stories may have been part of the universe of discourse which made it possible to recognize him as the Christ and whatever stories a combination of faith, imagination and realistic insight may now encourage us to tell on the basis of the wholly unmythological and realistic happenedness of Jesus.

Thus the notion of the Messiah is decisively demythologized, finally taken out of the realm of story and imagination, and embodied in materiality and history in the happenedness of a person. This means that it is perfectly proper to drop the usage 'Jesus the Messiah' where Messiah/Christ remains a title, and go over to the usage 'Jesus Christ' where the whole phrase is a proper name, designating the person who is the historical vindication and expression of what the story of God's dealings with men is truly about. But the happenedness of the person who is Jesus Christ does not only demythologize the notion of Messiah; it also universalizes it. For Jesus Christ lived a life and worked out a vocation which was brought to suffering, death and forsakenness. Representatives of his own people rejected his teaching and ministry as not only mistaken but evil, his few disciples forsook him and fled, and he himself in his dying moments provided evidence that he was passing through a sense of being forsaken by the God upon whom his whole life was orientated. Thus all that made up the personalness of Jesus was effectively and experientially brought to nothing, reduced beyond absurdity to apparent non-existence.

The discovery that this Jesus was the Christ lay the other side of this, through the experienced discovery of his risenness, of his resurrection. Jesus, therefore, may have been brought to nothing but he was not reduced to nothing. Rather he was now known to be Jesus Christ, the expression of the Kingdom of God. Hence everything which had brought him to nothing was inevitably put under the most decisive question mark. Divine reality lay with Jesus, and everything which stood against Jesus stood against divine reality. All the restrictions which confined God's interest to a particular set of people, which confined the hope of salvation to the performance of a certain pattern of rules or shut up the hope of forgiveness within loyalty to a particular tradition—indeed, all the restrictions which suggested that love was confined only to those who were in a certain defined way lovable, were decisively challenged. God stood with Jesus against all such. This is a lesson which has never yet been completely learned, and a fact which has never yet had its full practical appreciation. It is an expression of the universal openness of Jesus Christ which is itself the expression of the universal openness of the God who is transcendentally personal and loving, of which I shall seek to say more in the last lecture. But, although we may fall short of appreciating the implications of the fact and much further short of responding to the living applications of the fact, it remains clear that the actuality of the life of Jesus Christ declares the completely universal concern of God over against the restrictive and partial concerns of men, not least men of religion.

The way in which this universality of Jesus Christ, which is a declaration of the universal concern of God, was actually worked out is, of course, of decisive importance with regard to our concern for persons. I have been maintaining, I think with some reason, that we do not need to lose faith in the possibilities of personalness and that we are right to see in the observable realities and potentialities of human personalness a significant clue to the underlying reality of things. But in setting out my grounds for optimism I have so far largely avoided consideration of what, for many, is the most effective ground of pessimism. I refer to those experiences which men cannot but regard as unmitigated suffering and inexplicable evil. We are the subject of happenings some of which are so randomly ruthless in their effects on particular human beings and groups of human beings that we are inclined to think that the most, but cold, comfort that we can get is to judge that the happenings are *so* random, so meaningless and inexplicable, that we may at least conclude that it is nonsense to think of them as ruthless. They are just meaningless and evidence of meaninglessness. However, they do count most powerfully against any belief that there is a purpose and pattern behind, in and beyond the universe which is truly to be thought of as personal and concerned with persons.

I have little doubt that it is in the observable occurrence of meaningless evil and destructive suffering that there lies the most potent threat to the sustaining of any ultimate faith in the fitting together of men and the universe of which they are part in a manner which fulfils man. It is often alleged that the dimensions and complexities of the universe as they are becoming known to us through the investigation of science make it unthinkable that such a universe could be truly related to a transcendent concern which has at least one of its foci in a concern for the fulfilment of the humanness of men. But the allegation that the size of the universe makes it necessarily clear that it can have no ultimate personal significance is simply a mistake. This mistake has two forms, which lock into and reinforce one another. The first form is the logical muddle which confuses size with significance. It is the human mind which has the capacity to discover vastness and to analyze microscopic minuteness. There is no logic which forces this mind to derive from these discoveries and analyses which are its own work that which is destructive of its own significance. Scale, large or small, is a personally neutral feature of the universe.

This *logical* muddle, or rather the muddled belief that there is a compelling connection between size and significance, is reinforced by the *psychological* confusion which projects on to the vastness and complexity of the universe our own personal sense of aloneness. It is not size which deprives one of the awareness of personalness or of the hope of discovering personal purposes and patterns. It is the failure to make or develop truly personal relationships in the context of one's own life. Personal lostness and the depair of all hope of personal fulfilment do not derive from the restriction or expansion of the horizons of observation and investigation but from the inability to form reciprocal relationships with our neighbours. Love truly experienced and truly reciprocated can teach us to look confidently for personal possibilities and personal fulfilment over limitless space and time and through an infinitude of microscopic divisions.

But the question is whether love is to be found anywhere else than in man, and whether the love which man begins to know has any reflection in the universe as a whole or in any way underlies that universe. To this question the fiercely contra-personal and strictly contra-purposive aspects of evil encourage a negative answer which is not to be turned aside by the clarity of logic or by coming to terms with our psychological condition. Human experience is that there are aspects of the materiality and historicity of the universe which are not only indifferent to love but which are experienced as lying wholly against the grain of any pattern which men can recognizably relate to a pattern of love. How dare we therefore continue to maintain that the human and personal reality of man has any hope of finding response and fulfilment in and through the reality of the universe and the reality which underlies and goes beyond that universe?

We dare to do so because the intuitions and hopes which arise from our admittedly imperfect experience of being persons and from our admittedly imperfect knowledge of the achievements and possibilities of love are confronted with the discovery that the Logos of the cosmos is embodied in the personal actuality of Jesus Christ. The shape of this actuality was one of suffering, dying and forsakenness. The personalness of Jesus Christ was brought to nothing. The pattern which gives shape to the universe, the Logos which expresses the purpose and pattern of the transcendent and personal God, is lived out in materiality and history as a man who succumbs to suffering and evil. It is only beyond this involvement and identification to the point of submission to nothingness that there emerges the discovery of resurrection, of triumphant newness, of the vindication of the suffering and destroyed humanity of Jesus as the pattern of the power of the Kingdom of God. We do not see how the purposes of love can be reconciled with the purposelessness of evil, but we do see that the human being who embodies the pattern of the loving God is both submerged in the destructiveness of evil and emerges from it as a distinctive, living and personal activity. The Logos of the cosmos is not a mythological theory but a crucified man. The hope of personal sense and fulfilment lies neither in ignoring evil nor in explaining evil, but in the fact that Jesus Christ endured evil and emerged from evil.

It will be necessary in the final lecture to make some attempt at the temerarious task of speaking of the consequent revelation that we have here of the suffering of God. Here we are concerned with the reality of man. In Jesus Christ we have the demonstration that the true, human and personal reality of man is not submerged, defined nor ended by what I can only call the inexplicable and present reality of evil. The shape of the givenness of Jesus Christ is a shape which takes in the effect and fact of evil and yet emerges with human personalness intact. Thus we have grounds in the givenness of materiality and history for giving full rein to our belief and hope that the emergence and fulfilment of human personalness is at the heart of the personal purpose which underlies, and is at work in, materiality and history.

It may be that a fully Christian faith and understanding would be, or will be, able to go on to perceive that what I have characterized as 'meaningless evil' is not meaningless, i.e. does not counteract but in fact works with the grain of that pattern of things which leads to the fulfilment of persons. Indeed, this may be the plain implication of my own argument. I have been arguing that the things concerning Jesus show us that we are right to perceive a purpose at work which brings out of the stuff of materiality and history the pattern of personalness and, in the end, the fulfilment of persons. Now, just as this stuff of materiality and history produces, or is led to produce, what we recognize as persons, so it produces what strikes us as meaningless evil. If Jesus Christ really is the Logos of the cosmos, then must we not see the cosmos as a homogeneous and developing whole which, as whole, tends towards the development and fulfilment of persons? The interaction of fundamental particles according to the laws of probability or whatever it is that is to be considered as the basic 'stuff' of physical reality is that which produces both persons and the 'meaningless evil' which arises for them out of other physical features like earthquakes, cancer and so on. Since we have grounds, in the reality of Jesus Christ and in the reality of persons, for holding that the processes are both patient of and productive of personal purposes, and also will be led to the fulfilment of personal purposes, then we must conclude that the processes are not meaningless and, therefore, that what strikes us as meaningless evil cannot be so.

As I say, I am inclined to believe that a fully Christian understanding of things (i.e. an understanding that was in full accordance with the reality of Jesus Christ) would develop in this direction.

Indeed some such development is probably demanded if we are to avoid dualism—the absurd understanding of the ultimate existence of two sorts of reality one of which is personally good and the other of which is intrinsically evil. However, I do not have a fully Christian understanding. I am at present trying to follow the argument wherever it leads, while very well aware that one can be only at a certain stage of this sort of argument with views about its ultimate direction and a varied assortment of loose ends, some stimulating, some frustrating and some frightening. In practice it seems sufficiently clearly the human lot to encounter and suffer from much that goes against the grain of humanity and personalness. As such, we experience it as meaningless evil and we have to see what the things concerning Jesus have to say to this situation. We may, I am sure, believe and hope that there is much more to be said than we have yet discerned, but we cannot effectively push the logic of the argument we believe we discern beyond what we find existentially and psychologically acceptable. For myself, therefore, I am clear that Jesus Christ enables us humanly and hopefully to face evil. I do not yet see that he enables us to explain evil.

But Jesus Christ is not only the demonstration of the ultimate possibility of the emergence and fulfilment of personalness, he is also the definition of the nature of personalness. It is in and through the givenness of the man Jesus Christ that we can at last give some precise outline to the notion of personalness which I have so far been making play the ambiguous rôle of a given which is both decisive and yet undefined. The personalness to be outlined is that which is to be seen in or hoped for in human beings. What may be said about the personalness of God must be considered in the next and last lecture.

Jesus Christ shows that a truly human person, a real man, is an individual who is wholly and consistently open to all the possibilities of materiality and history as they impinge upon him, to all the demands and possibilities of other persons as he encounters them, and to the reality of God which is both involved in materiality, historicity and other persons and also exists independently and transcendentally. Such a real man has never yet existed save in the defining case of Jesus Christ, but this is the reality of which all men to some extent partake, for which all men are destined and in which all men will find the complete fulfilment of their existence. It is human 'nature', all that is involved in being a man. But this nature is not something static, substantial, fixed. Rather it is an emergent and emerging pattern. The possibility of this pattern emerging and obtaining fulfilment out of the impersonal processes and patterns of the material universe and out of the events of history, patterned, patternless or destructive, lies in the antecedent fact of the transcendent and independent existence of the personal God and the consequent fact of the union of derived and emergent personalness with the divine personalness. The evidence for this understanding of the emerging process and final pattern of human personalness is focused on Jesus Christ, but supporting evidence is to be obtained from all those features of human existence which on reasonable investigation support the case for finding anthropology opening into theology.

The reality of man is to be understood in the light of the fact that the universe as created, that is, known in relation to the transcendent God, is material for purposive and personal living. Both history and matter can be *ordered* by human understanding, action and reaction to produce purpose and life which derives from humanness and enhances humanness. This is something which was uniquely discovered by the prophetic insight of inspired Israelites and Jews. Jeremiah and others, for example, discovered that the inner purpose and reality of history was to be perceived not in the destruction of Jerusalem but in the re-birth of the Jewish community. Creative human possibilities arise out of inhuman and chaotic happenings because there is always the possibility of response to the God who transcends every happening as well as every thing.

This prophetic insight was a God-given discernment of the way in which God's purposes of personal fulfilment are to be produced out of the stuff of materiality and history by the response of men to God. This response is a real and creative one made on the basis of God's initiative, sustained by God's creative presence, and consummated by God's decisive fulfilment. This way of God's working is recognized as men learn that there is a power other than the powers of the material processes which produce things and the historical interactions which produce events. This power, as far as men are concerned, is discernible in and through things and happenings but it is not the power of the things and happenings themselves, and it sets men free to overcome and transcend the impersonal forces of the things and happenings so that personal purposes and possibilities can be woven out of what is basically impersonal and even, apparently, contra-personal.

This crucial matter requires much more extended treatment than I can give it here but I may, perhaps, pause briefly on the one illustration I have mentioned. Is there any decisive factor which essentially differentiates the destruction of Jerusalem by the Babylonians from any overthrow of an independent small state by a neighbouring empire whether it be, say, in the Middle East, Far East or South America? Surely the answer as far as the materiality and historicity of the event goes must be 'No'. Famine, fear, bereavement, enslavement and exile have the same physical features everywhere and expansion and conquest are common historical phenomena. These features and phenomena present everywhere the same obliterating threats to humanness and the life of individuals as well as manifesting the same 'laws' both of materiality and of history. But in the case of the fall of Jerusalem, the involvement and response of such men as Jeremiah, Ezekiel and the author or authors of passages in the book of Isaiah now critically referred to as 'deutero-Isaiah', produced a unique discernment in, and interpretation of, the happenings which had perceptible consequences.

They saw in the events which led up to, constituted, and followed from the destruction of Jerusalem the hand and purpose of God. Thus the central and decisive happening was not the physical sequence of siege, famine, assault, death and exile, real and harrowing as it was. Nor was it the successful expansion of Nebuchadnezzar's Babylonian empire, historically real and influential as this was. Rather the central and decisive happening was the judgement of God upon his faithless people. Because of this, there did not occur that disappearance of the people who believed in their covenanted relation to the true and the living God which would have falsified the truth-claim implied in their belief. Rather, through and beyond the destruction and exile which was discerned as containing the judgement of God, there came the emergence of the Kingdom of Judah re-born as the people of the Jews, ready for the next stages of the encounter with, discernment of, and response to the true and living God.

The prophetic insight and inspiration was so to read God's purpose into materiality and history that it became possible to produce God's purpose out of materiality and history. But both the prophetic insight and the personal possibility depend primarily on the antecedent existence of the God who has personal purposes for materiality and history, and on the consequent fact that materiality and history thus lie available for personal ordering where there is responsive and responsible co-operation between God and man. By this co-operation between man and God, the possibilities of development into personal purposes which lie latent in the stuff of materiality and history because that stuff is basically 'created' actually emerge and are recognized by those persons who are themselves being formed by and yet emerging out of this same stuff. Thus men both are emergent persons and are the agents of emergent personal purposes. By discerning what is partially and potentially present, they have the opportunity to assist in its creative realization.

The persons who were led to give a clear expression to this vital clue to the pattern and possibilities of the universe in which men live, from which men emerge, and of which they are a homogeneous but potentially transcendent part, were the inspired prophets of the people who became the Jews. Their insight emerged within history and made its contribution to history. This contribution is not yet fulfilled, both in the sense that history is not yet fulfilled and in the sense that men have not yet seen all that is implied by and results from this contribution. To follow in the logic and in the power of the prophetic discernment demands a continuing openness to new understandings and new responses learnt from the present realities of materiality and history, an openness and discernment corresponding to that of the prophets themselves.

One type of openness and discernment which today corresponds in at least one vital respect to that of the prophets is that shown in the valid practice of science. There is a close and non-accidental analogy between the prophetic insight of which I have been speaking and the way in which science gives order to materiality. In practice, science and its consequent technology has led to a vast increase in the ability of men to order materiality for purposes of personal living. Here again (cf. Lecture VI, p. 61) it is not a question of claiming that the prophetic insight as historically expressed leads through the historical expressions of Christianity to the causal developments of science and technology. Rather it is to point out that science and technology now provide a vast extension of practical evidence that the stuff of the universe is patient of ordering by persons for personal purposes. In this, I am arguing, we are to see a further and, until it occurred, undreamed-of vindication of the prophetic insight that history and matter can be ordered by human understanding for humanness.

But the pattern of the development of personalness is the pattern of response to personalness. Unless man develops his derived personal reality in response to the underived personal reality of God, he loses his personalness in the impersonalness of the dependent materiality and history out of which he is emerging and in which he is either growing towards personalness or losing the chance of personalness. The pattern and purpose which encourages and fulfils personalness must transcend the processes of materiality and the pattern of history or it is their fragmentariness, unfinishedness and impersonalness which must be determinative. Jesus Christ, however, makes it clear that the last word and the ultimate hope lies with the emergent pattern of personalness, because these immanent developments are the intimate concern of the transcendentally personal. So we are to see the reality of man in the light of the direction in which he is developing, a direction of ever increasing possibilities of freedom, openness, and involvement with the potentialities both of the universe at large and of human beings among themselves. But this reality is both a developing reality and a dependent reality, developing from and dependent on materiality and history on the one hand, and dependent for fulfilment on development towards God on the other. There is no dichotomy between these two types of dependence and development, but there is a distinction, and if man fails to distinguish God from everything else then he loses his practical understanding of the true reality of everything else and of himself with it.

Personalness, therefore, is the self-conscious, open and characteristically human pattern which is to be found potentially and in varying degrees of development in each individual of the human species. This pattern has emerged out of the processes and patterns of the universe, and has the unique distinction of being both wholly rooted in the stuff of the universe and of reaching out beyond it. In the developing patterns of personalness the processes and patterns of the universe take on meaning and purpose. Further, what personalness itself requires for fulfilment is a fulfilling pattern and purpose. This fulfilment lies in the original and final transcendent personalness who is God. You cannot define the reality of man, the human person, without taking into account the reality of God.

But Jesus Christ makes it clear that this way of understanding the world, man and God is not anthropomorphism. It is true that man has always tended to see God in his (i.e. man's) own image. But God has not allowed man to rest in any idolatry, partial theism or false atheism, for God cares for man and will not leave him to the mercy of any impersonal forces, least of all those active in himself. Thus, in Jesus Christ, we are finally confronted with God taking on man's own, true and real image. In this historical presentation of the one fully real man we are confronted with the reality of the one true God. We have, therefore, to consider in the last lecture how we are finally and decisively prevented from thinking of God in our own image because God has finally and decisively made the human image his own.

VIII

True God

JESUS CHRIST IS the reality of man who confronts us with the reality of God. That is to say, firstly, that the historical person whose name was Jesus and who is now rightly designated Jesus Christ lived a life which brought to actual concrete expression in terms of particular materiality and historicity all that is necessary for the development of a complete man. All that is involved in thus being a man is that one is a particular personal individual, homogeneous in origin with the rest of the stuff of the universe, who emerges out of that stuff into the possibility of personalness through the particularity of the materiality and historicity of ones own origin and circumstances. The developing personal pattern who is a man has to mature and fulfil his particular personalness in openness to all surrounding materiality, historicity and personality. To bring all that is involved in being a man to the fulfilled possibilities of being a person in this way, it is necessary to be wholly open to the transcendent personalness of God, who is to be known both in and through all the surrounding circumstances and in himself. Thus Jesus Christ is all that is involved in being a man in that he emerges as every man must emerge and is involved as every man must be involved, and also in that the pattern of his living both is and achieves the perfect integration of his personalness in and through his perfect union with God.

In this matter of perfect integration of self and perfect union with God, Jesus Christ is all that is involved in being a man in the sense that he achieves, and is, all that it is necessary for a man to become if he is to achieve the fulfilment of the reality of his human personalness. Thus he is literally the one true man in the sense that he is the one so far existent example of what man must come to if he is to fulfil his humanness, and of what man will come to because God is concerned to achieve that fulfilment. In this way Jesus Christ is 'perfect in manhood', complete in his human nature, all that is involved in being a man. He is different from all other men only in the sense that he is the fulfilled achievement of that process and pattern which constitutes, in its various individualizations, the distinctive human existence of every man and in the case of every other man, that fulfilment which is yet to come.

It is in this sense of providing the historical example of the actualization and fulfilment of that pattern which is the pattern which will give fulfilment to every human being, that Jesus Christ may be said to be 'perfect in manhood' or to 'have human nature'. The 'nature' language is to be retained as standing for the distinctive and defining pattern which makes up and completes a fulfilled human person—all that is eventually and ultimately involved in being a man.

He is the living dynamic pattern and process which defines and constitutes his own person in the fulfilling way which every personal individuality must achieve if he or she is to be fulfilled. To point towards the completion of the picture it is highly significant and necessary to notice that the Christian hope is that the pattern of the one perfect man will be shared by all men so that in the end humanity as a whole will have its fulfilment 'in Christ'. But within the compass of the argument of these particular lectures there is no space to pursue the practical, social and splendid implications of this for our understanding of what it is, what it can be and what it will be to be a man in relation to every man and to God. We must rest with our statement that Jesus Christ is all that is involved in being a man, demonstrates and defines the nature all men share in, are developing and need to have fulfilled. (But see slightly further the postscript pp. 161 f.)

Secondly, this truly real man confronts us with the reality of God. As I have said, divine reality lay with Jesus. The Resurrection vindicated all that Jesus stood for in relation to the Kingdom of God. His livingness on the other side of his death made it clear that his original livingness represented the way God does things under the conditions of materiality and history in order to draw out of materiality and history his transcendent and personal purposes. Thus it becomes clear that the shape of the personalness of Jesus Christ is the embodied shape of the pattern of the personalness of God. The human Jesus Christ is what the divine God does, and what God does is to express himself as the man Jesus Christ in the conditions of materiality and history so that his purposes for materiality and history can be realized. As I have already said (Lecture V, p. 55), in Jesus Christ there is discovered the personal fulfilment both of God and of man.

But when we say that Jesus Christ is the personal fulfilment of man we mean something different from what we mean when we say that he is the personal fulfilment of God, although we are using both phrases correctly and fully of one and the same person, i.e. of Jesus Christ himself. This is so because God and man are distinct realities who, in and as Jesus Christ, are in perfect union. We are discussing here the Chalcedonian 'shape', viz. two distinct and perfect natures in perfect personal union.

The nature of man is to be an individual who, in a series of relationships, is a developing personal pattern recognizable as a dynamic continuation of a process of emergence and growth. Thus the personal fulfilment of man is when the individual personal pattern reaches a mature wholeness which finds fulfilment in the full expression and enjoyment of personalness in relation to the transcendent and inexhaustible personalness of God. Jesus Christ is the personal fulfilment of man in the sense that he achieved, expressed and enjoyed that full expression of personalness under conditions of materiality and history. Before Jesus Christ the fulfilment of man had never been achieved, and he is the fulfilment into which all men have the opportunity of entering.

The nature of God is to be God and we have to be very careful about saying anything more. But we may combine the whole teaching of the experience underlying the Bible about the unchangeable reliability of God with what we have discovered about the loss of the possibilities of personalness if they are found only in process and change, to reiterate from the whole theistic tradition that it is the nature of God to transcend all change and process and to be steadfast and complete in his being as God, free from any need of, or danger of, change. Thus to speak of the personal fulfilment of God is not to be saying that God has for the first time come into the possession and enjoyment of the full potentialities of his nature. It is to say that God has for the first time achieved under the conditions of materiality and history that full expression of the pattern of his personal purposes which expresses that in his nature which relates him to the whole cosmic process. We have God expressing his true and eternal self in the form which is appropriate to the conditions provided by the dependent and developing universe. Man has to achieve his fullness as man. God is always his fullness as God, but he does set himself to achieve his expression of this fullness in the midst of the processes and happenings of the universe in relation to the fulfilment of the purposes which spring from his fullness.

We have to set ourselves to consider the implications of the discovered fact that the human being who is Jesus Christ is the appropriate expression of the reality of God and see what effect this has on our understanding of the reality of God. We must, of course, be quite clear that there is one very important sense in which we cannot understand the reality of God. We cannot understand all that is involved in his being God, nor can we expect to understand, if I may so put it, why he is God or how he can succeed in being God. We must be content to accept the mystery of his being God because we have had kindled in us the faith and the awareness that he is God, that there is open to us the possibility of a reciprocity of relationship with him who is beyond anything and everything with which we have to do, but who none the less is concerned to have to do with us. Because he is concerned to have to do with us there are offered to us ways of understanding his reality, both that he is and also what is the true significance of his existence as far as we are concerned. But because it is God who has to do with us, we must be careful not to suppose that there is open to us an understanding of what might be called the structure of his nature and the articulation of his workings. In particular we must not imagine that we can expose, and satisfy ourselves about, the method or methods of his Incarnation.

Thus the position which I have tried to argue towards and set out, and which I believe to be required by the Christian understanding of the things concerning Jesus is as follows. We may know that Jesus is the Christ. We may also know that Jesus Christ is the historical presentation of the pattern, power and purpose of God. We of course know that Jesus Christ is human and that he is one person, himself and not someone else. We further know that God is God and, as such, distinct from everything else. To hold all this together we are obliged to say that Jesus Christ, as the person he is, is the personal union of God and man, the perfection of union of two distinct perfections. We are not called upon to explain *how* this can be so before we can maintain it, because we are not in a position to start from some theory about God and theory about man which will give us the clues and grounds for such an explanation. We are not theorizing at all. We are responding to recognizable givenness. Now we have to see what this givenness implies, how we are thereby required to understand the reality of man and the truth about God as far as understanding is open to us.

What then are we to understand about the reality of God in the light of the discovery that the human being who is Jesus Christ is the historically appropriate expression of this reality? Above all, surely, that the expression 'God is love' is no mere manner of speaking nor simply the sincere expression of a pious hope. The pattern of the personalness of the real man and the pattern of the personalness of the true God perfectly coincide, for Jesus Christ is the one integrated person who, in his historical actuality, is constituted by and as these patterns. Jesus Christ is one person, one integrated personality, one pattern of personalness. But this pattern is the pattern of the real man and the pattern of the true God, that is to say it is both human nature and divine nature. But God as transcendent and independent is necessarily distinct from man as emergent and dependent, as far as nature or defining reality goes. Nevertheless in Jesus Christ we have a real person, one pattern of personalness. It would seem, therefore, as I have just said, that in Jesus Christ the personal pattern of man and the personal pattern of God coincide.

But on reflection this suggestion, this attempted unfolding of the insight of faith, does not begin to be adequate to the reality presented to us. An integrated personality is not the coincidence of two patterns of personalness. An integrated personality is the fulfilled and fulfilling expression of one pattern of personalness. We can, however, I believe, begin to have some insight into the mystery which is the reality of one integrated personality, one fulfilled pattern of personalness, being the full personal expression of two patterns of personalness. This is the mystery of love. It is *not* the mystification arising from loose talk about love. Still less is it the muddle arising from romantic escapism indulging in fantasies about love. We are concerned with the concrete presentation of the mystery which is love in action, seen in its fullness in the embodiment of God as the crucified man, Jesus Christ, and experienced in its beginnings, at its fringes as we might say, by every human being who has begun to share his or her essential personal reality with another in the first faltering steps of the interchange of love.

As I think I might perhaps be beginning to understand it, I glimpse somewhat as follows. Jesus Christ is the purposive and personal pattern of God and man in union. The shape of the personalness of his human life was the obedience and service of love, love which is, and which comes from, full openness to God and full openness to one's neighbour. Real man is in existence when there is perfect, freely given, and therefore fully personal, obedience to the two commandments of loving God with the whole of one's personality and of loving one's neighbour with the full openness with which a fully integrated personality is open to the realities of his or her own self. In such a fully personal and open expression of love the two commandments are fulfilled in such a way that they cease to be commandments, for such love is not in any way the result of, or related to, the pressure of an external command, but is the wholly spontaneous expression of the personality concerned. Thus in Jesus Christ as far as his humanity goes, we have the perfection of the obedience of love and of the service of love which is the perfect expression of the fulfilled and fulfilling pattern of human personalness. This is what men are 'for', and this is how they are to enjoy and fulfil being themselves, by being and expressing what they are for, namely the reciprocity of the openness of love.

But the full, fulfilled and fulfilling reciprocity of the openness of love is not to be found among men as yet. Where Jesus found it, and what enabled Jesus humanly to express it unwaveringly despite the lack of adequate human response, was in the openness of the love of God. The pattern of the human personalness of Jesus was determined by the obedience of love expressed in the service of love. This was perfectly matched by the pattern of the divine personalness which is transcendent love likewise expressed, in relation to materiality and history, as the service of love. If I may be allowed to strive after crude simplicity of expression for so high a matter, which if it is true, must be profoundly simple, I would say that what we are to learn is that when the love of God and the love of man really get down to it they come to the same thing. Or, rather, since love is so highly personal and personalness is so bound up with love, we should better say that when God who is truly love, and man who can find his true reality only in love, get down, in the stuff of materiality and history, to expressing their true selves, it comes to the same person. Thus Jesus Christ is the person who is the perfect coincidence of the pattern of personalness determined by the human service of love and that determined by the divine service of love. But because we are confronted with the coincidence of patterns of personalness which are determined and defined by love, we do not encounter coincidence but personal union. God *is* the loving man. The man *is* the loving God. There is through perfect love the perfect interchange of existence which is the height and depth of personal union. The existence of Jesus Christ depends wholly on the living God while the existence of Jesus Christ is expressed wholly as the loving man. We may not and we cannot divide the person, the personality or the personalness. But we may and we must understand that the personal union is a union of distinctness which depends for the very possibility of its existence on the initial, independent and transcendent existence of God who is personally and purposively concerned to unite emergent, dependent and fulfilled human personalness to himself.

Whatever may be made of this attempt of mine to make one more halting contribution to the contemplation of the mystery with which the givenness of Jesus confronts us, I feel bound to follow up certain ideas which it suggests concerning our proper and legitimate understanding of God. I am sure that we have now left the realms of incisive logical argument and I would myself judge that we are also very near, if not beyond, the limits of the realms of even tentative dogmatic definition. But I remain convinced that there is yet a realm wherein we may, with fear and trembling mingled with hope and joy, expect to be able to delineate certain perceptions which have some reasonable chance of being insights into the mystery of God in which men are called to partake.

Consider the conclusion, *à propos* of Jesus Christ, that God is the loving man, the man is the loving God. This makes it clear that it is perfectly possible for the reality of the transcendent God to be expressed as a function of, and in terms of, total involvement in the processes of materiality and the events of history. Doubtless we are to be clear that such a total involvement is possible only when materiality has reached the level of personalness, but at that level we are shown that there is no contradiction in actuality between the divine transcendence and immanence. No matter what theistic theories may have held to be the case, it is clear that in practice, that is in the practical exercise by God of his divine personalness in relation to the stuff out of which we emerge, there is no contradiction between transcendence and immanence, between being wholly other and being wholly involved, between being completely free of all necessary attachments to anything else and being completely committed to everything else. The absolute freedom of God, wherein he transcends and is detached from everything else, is no bar to his total involvement in and concern for all the personal possibilities of the universe because as he is absolutely free so he is absolutely love. It thus becomes quite clear that the tendency in much current theological debate to oppose transcendence to immanence or insist on substituting involvement language for all detachment language is simply a mistake arising out of a combination of misunderstanding and ignorance of the authentic implications of the authentic Christian tradition. It is a mistake too, as I hope I have shown in earlier lectures, which is destructive of man via the demotion of God. Transcendence without immanence makes nonsense of God, immanence without transcendence makes nonsense of man. Both are quite untrue to the givenness of Jesus Christ.

The givenness of the personalness of Jesus Christ is, then, the givenness of the personalness of God in terms of materiality and history. This presents us not only with the involvement of God in process and event, but also with the identification of God with the suffering man. The personal involvement which expresses the pattern of the personalness of the loving God leads to that expression of the divine which is the suffering and dying man. This is an extension of the mystery of the union of love which is certainly very hard to accept, let alone to begin to understand, but I believe it to be undeniable. God expresses himself as the man who suffers, is forsaken and dies.

Attempts have been made to explain, mitigate and, in effect, to deny this mystery by various uses of the concept of *kenosis*, of the notion of the emptying out of the divine in the Incarnation, to which there is some sort of reference in what is probably a very early Christian hymn made use of by Paul in the second chapter of his letter to the Philippians. These attempts, when they go beyond being poetic references or perceptive uses of language which attempt to pass on partial but sometimes penetrating insights, make it abundantly clear that the pursuit of detailed expositions of the method of the Incarnation or of the articulation of the divine and human in Jesus Christ are useless if they are not harmful. The language of emptying is already referring to the expression of the divine love in the historical reality of Jesus Christ, and cannot be used as if it enables us further to unpack that mystery. It does, however, help to point us, not to what lies behind and so makes possible the mystery, but to what the mystery actually shows us.

This is, as far as I can see it and put it, that God is perfectly willing, and therefore able, to give himself away in the furtherance of his purposes of love which are themselves the expression of the pattern of his personalness. The man Jesus Christ who is the embodiment of the pattern of the personalness of God is brought to nothing. He is not thereby reduced to nothing because he is the expression of the transcendent and omnipotent God. But this transcendent omnipotence is the power of absolute love which finds true expression in going out from the pattern of personalness wholly into and wholly for the other. This is not to give love away nor to empty out what it is to be divine, but rather to give expression to what it is to be divine, to be love. Hence the bringing to nothingness is not the final reduction to nothingness but the completion of that identification which is the triumphant and free work of love whereby love works forward to fulfilment at any costs and through any odds. In so far as we can glimpse the true meaning and the true power of love, I believe we can glimpse the possibility of the mystery that God expresses himself as the suffering, forsaken and dying man. In relation to the practical problem of evil, God is neither indifferent, ncompetent nor defeated. He is involved, identified and inevitably triumphant.

The involvement of the transcendent God in our stuff of materiality and history gives us hope. But the identification of God with the suffering, dying and forsaken man must give us pause. I do not, however, think that we may finally turn aside, however much we may shrink, from attempting to face the fact that God suffers. The embodiment of the pattern of personalness of God is the pattern of the personalness of Jesus Christ. The reality of this latter pattern is suffused with suffering. There can be no reality in the union of pattern and personalness unless suffering has a real place in the pattern of the personalness of God. The givenness of Jesus Christ surely demands that we try to understand that the love of God is not condescension but compassion. The question mark which evil suffering places upon the existence of man in the world and the whole meaningful existence of the universe has superimposed upon it the Cross, as the expression in materiality and history of God's real and true openness to all the suffering which seems, as matter of observable but inexplicable facts, to be concomitant with the emergence of his purposes. Since God suffers, and God is God, we are not left with the absurdity wherein evil and suffering emerge as the indifferent randomness which destroys all meaning, nor are we left with a perhaps even more terrifying and more nonsensical dualism in which a divine goodness struggles in a precariously matched eternal conflict with a contradictory yet equally divine evil. Rather we are confronted with the opportunity of faith in, and knowledge of, the God who secures the hope of the fulfilment of derived personalness by accepting, absorbing and transforming all that is contrary to it.

But the fact must be faced that to take this line is to invite an atheistic retort which would have much support, although from a different viewpoint, from within the theistic tradition. The retort is 'If God suffers, then surely he is not God'. The atheistic point of this retort is the conclusion that there is, after all, no God. The theistic point is the conclusion that in the last analysis God does not suffer. My own judgement would be that it might be nearer the mark to make the counter-retort 'Unless God suffers, there is no God'. For if God does not suffer, but produces his purposes out of suffering by a divine condescension proceeding from absolute detachment, then it is exceedingly difficult to see how he can be regarded as other than a cosmic monster. On the other hand, the notion that God has let himself in for involvement in suffering would seem to have its futility best thrown into relief by saying that such a notion justifies the wry and near blasphemous comment that God is a fool—and a cosmic fool at that. At any rate it is very clear that we have the whole notion of God at risk.

I see nowhere else to turn in all this than to the givenness of Jesus Christ, which is, no doubt, simply to say that I am a Christian. Here I see that, indeed, everything is at risk. The man whose givenness I see reason to understand as the embodied givenness of God passes through an experience which he interprets as God-forsakenness. I believe that this is to be seen as evidence that God enters into the experience of that in the universe which counts for atheism. Thereby it is shown that it need not so count but that it can be brought within the scope of the purposes of personalness and love. Thus we are confronted with a God in whom it is possible to believe when living in a world with the sort of materiality and history that is actually known to us. If, however, we conclude that God has taken too big a risk, we shall not believe in him. We shall, however, still be confronted with the givenness of Jesus and with the dimension of personalness.

Thus I cannot escape the conclusion that the true God, as he is seen through Jesus Christ, must be understood to be truly open to the suffering of the world. We are free, therefore, both to rest in his compassion and to be shaped by his compassion into a passionate attack on all that adds to suffering or stands in the way of its mitigation and transformation. Love is no idle word, the love of God is no idle force, and those who would wish to be counted as lovers of God can never rest content with indifferent or cowardly idleness. Moreover I do not believe that an understanding of the reality of the God who is love along the lines I am diffidently suggesting in fact runs counter to the authentic insight contained within the traditional theistic notion of the impassibility of God.

God, it has always been held by those who have understood and experienced believing in God as response to existent and authentic reality, does not change. He is not at the mercy of events and things for his existence as God nor for the enjoyment and expression of his essential reality as God. Whatever his relationship to continuing processes and developing patterns, he himself is not to be equated with those processes and patterns, and he is not dependent for his being God, or his being as God, in any way on the movements, developments, changes in materiality and history. This insight into the transcendent independence of God in his godness is, I am convinced, a valid one. The God who is nothing but involvement is not the God of biblical encounter nor the God of theistic worship nor the God who is required by, and the fulfilment of, the mystery of personalness and love. The God who is necessary to the fulfilment of the mystery of love cannot exist *because* he is this fulfilment, nor *in order to* be that fulfilment, nor *in so far as* that fulfilment comes into being. Rather, the possibility of love and personalness emerges, and the fulfilment of personalness and love is realistically to be looked for, because or in so far as God exists in his transcendental personalness antecedently to and independently of these possibilities. God does not exist in order to guarantee man fulfilment. Such a notion is idolatrous anthromorphism. Nor is authentic belief in the living God man's projection on to the universe of his unrealistic determination to hold, contrary to reality, that there is a possibility of his fulfilment. We are rapidly gaining sufficient psychological insights to dissipate that sort of fantasy and to enable us to move into a clarity in which it will emerge whether there is a true God or not. The true God exists because he is the true God and it is a *consequence* of his transcendentally independent existence both that man exists and that man has the hope of fulfilment as man.

God, therefore, depends only and wholly upon himself for the totality and fulfilment of his existence as God. This means that he must be understood as having no necessary relations with any thing or person other than himself. The relations are not necessary because God in no way depends on them for being God. But this has been usually taken to imply that if God does choose to establish relations with something other than himself then these relations can *make no difference to him.* If his being in relationship to the universe and to men makes a difference to God, then he either depends on the effect of these relations to enable him to become more truly God, or he succumbs to the effect of these relations by becoming less truly God. In either case he is then shown to be not God but simply a function of the universe. Hence the godness of God is held to require an understanding of his transcendent independence which excludes the possibility of any of his real relations with the universe and men making any difference to him, and this has been expressed as his impassibility, as his being out of the reach of all experience and suffering which could make any difference to or have any effect upon him.

In the light, however, of the experience of God which builds up to the recognition of Jesus Christ as the embodiment of the pattern of God's personalness, it would seem that we are required to interpret our understanding of what is involved in God's transcendent existence in a somewhat different way to that normally associated with the notion of impassibility. We have to build into our understanding of the godness of God the implications of the fact that we are confronted with evidence of God's practical capacity for involvement and identification. As I have felt obliged to suggest, this must produce the conclusion that God suffers. I would reiterate the suggestion that this is indeed so but that the suffering of God does not make any difference to his being God. For neither the Bible, nor Jesus Christ, nor our experience and understanding of what is involved in personalness, supports the notion that we are to conceive of the perfection of God, or of any personalness, as the perfect union of a set of static attributes which can, so to speak, be knocked off their pinnacles of perfection by something happening to them. Rather we have revealed to us something much more like a dynamically active pattern which is to be appreciated in terms of love and loving.

I would suggest that we can at least entertain the notion that fully personal love and fully loving personalness might be absolutely capable of being completely open to all the effects resulting from any relations whatever without this making any difference at all to the nature, pattern, purpose and effectiveness of this love. I would sum up the point I am trying to make here by saying that the notion of the impassibility of God stands for the fact that God is in no way dependent on anything outside himself for being himself, and that further, and most importantly, nothing whatever can put him off being God. He is the Lord and he does not change. But he has made it known to us that the energy which manifests the essence of his being, in so far as manifestation is possible, is the energy of love. His unchangeability, therefore, is unquenchable love which can and does suffer everything at a deeper level of fully personal experience than is either open to or endurable for any of us, but this makes not one iota of difference to the reality of this love. The experienced reality of the Cross has to be seen as pointing to the centre of what it means to God to be God, but this is no threat to his unchangeable and imperishable divinity. It is the very expression of it, whereby the power of his personalness is made overwhelmingly effective for all men without the individual personalness of any single man being thereby overwhelmed. For to be taken up by personal love which is expressed in terms of complete openness, identification and compassion to the point of irresistible union is not to be swallowed up but to be set free to be yourself, in union with God and with every other loved and loving self.

But, it may be urged, all this is only a vision, a possible perspective, a personal hope. So it is. But it is a vision which has strong claims to have elements of true insight arising from the givenness of Jesus Christ rooted in materiality and events, arising also from the observed givenness of personalness and renewed in the continually experienced givenness of the possibilities which arise out of and in connection with the worship of God. The vision is, however, always obscured when the worship is obscured. For it is in worship that one is faced with both the offer and the demand of transcendence, of the immeasurable distance which goes with the intimate closeness of the living God whose life is love. Worship is the way of experiencing the infinite openness of the possibilities of the personal. And this openness is, as far as we are concerned, the practice of the response of love to the love of the God who in the infinite openness of his love is endlessly and gloriously worshipful. There is no end to the possibilities of being human, but this openness is joy and hope, not weariness and despair, for the endless possibilities exist already in and as the glory of God.

But we shall never progress, indeed we shall scarcely begin, in the true worship of the true God which is the way to the fulfilment of man, unless we look for the grace to be truly scientific. Our investigation into the givenness of Jesus Christ has surely made one thing clear. To be human and personal is to be open to whatever is given, to all data. We are in the image of God, but this describes our potentialities more than our present realities. Thus we must not anthropomorphically think of God in *our* image. That is, we must not be trapped in any symbol, picture or definition of God. The *image* we have of God, still less the image we have of ourselves, is never decisively definitive of our commitment to our true reality, which is to be fulfilled in the reality of the transcendent and inexhaustible God. Similarly, no present theory of the universe must finally shut in our developing understanding of that universe, of our place within it, and of the reality of the God who is making us for himself in and through the stuff of that universe. The insight of the vision which Jesus Christ offers us will be lost unless we put into practice whatever insight we so far have by a continually open investigation of all that is presented to us and by a willingness to respond to every new imperative which such investigation throws up for us.

We are not sufficiently personal as yet to practice such openness by ourselves, but if we are to become fully and truly personal we need such openness for ourselves. Our hope lies in the evidence of Jesus Christ that the openness we need is offered to us by and as the openness of the love of God. We need be trapped in no mythology, no theory, and in no fragmentation of absurdity. We have, rather, the opportunity of hopeful openness in the fearless development of science and in the loving development of personalness. Both come together in the worship of the transcendent God and in dependence upon the immanent God.

Even if there has seemed to be some coherence and force in some part of my argument as I have tried to unfold it, you will still surely ask, 'But what does this mean?'. This is what you should ask and what we must always ask. If it is true that the fulfilment of our human personalness lies in union with the personalness of God, then we can never in this life suppose that we have reached the end of meaningfulness. Jesus Christ is a sufficient statement of our hope and definition of our direction. God will not let us go back on what has been said in him about the possibilities and fulfilment of love and personalness. But the meaning of the following of Jesus Christ does not now lie in resting in indicatives. It is to be discovered in the obedient response to imperatives and in the hopeful facing of questions.

The Question of Truth

I HAVE BEEN attempting to argue for the truth of Christianity in the sense that I have been seeking a reconsideration of the truth about God and about man which is implied by Jesus. I have not been attempting to show by argument 'that Christianity is true', whatever precisely would be meant by that phrase. I must hope that the lectures do reflect and convey my conviction that the things concerning Jesus are of central and decisive importance in putting us on to the realities of man's situation with regard to the world and God. Since I suffer from the further conviction that reality must be faced, I naturally believe and desire that others should see and be convinced of those realities about God and man which are demonstrated in Jesus and pointed to by Jesus. This desire of mine is reinforced by the evident fact that what is declared about reality by and through Jesus is realistic and practical good news about the possibilities and direction of human fulfilment. The things concerning Jesus constitute and imply a universal Gospel the contents of which are so humanly worthwhile that it would demonstrate the extreme of inhumanity not to wish urgently to share this good news. Hence I find myself under precisely the same command and obligation to 'preach the gospel' as did the Christians of New Testament times.

I do not believe, however, that the truth, even when it is good news which points towards a glory greater than we can so far comprehend, is something which can be forced upon people. Indeed, 'the truth as it is in Jesus' surely underlines this point. For he established the reality of his person, his mission and his message through identification and beyond death in a manner which displayed faith and love rather than enforced submission. The truth which concerns persons, if, as Jesus demonstrates, it is to do with the fulfilment of persons, must remain personal and free and cannot compel impersonal acquiescence. Moreover, seeing that this truth is to do with the fulfilment of the potentialities of men in the reality of God, it becomes clearer than ever that it is truth which cannot be established but must establish itself. God cannot be manipulated by or established upon lesser realities than himself.

Hence it is possible to argue for the truths involved in the things concerning Jesus only by looking to see what those truths are, investigating them and seeking to respond to them. Christian truth must be essentially experiential and experimental and always as much a hope as a possession. This is simply to say that 'Christians', i.e. those consciously concerned to respond to the things concerning Jesus, are by this very concern required to follow a way of authentic involvement with serial reality rather than to take refuge in what is believed to be a castle, but turns out to be a cage, of enforceable dogma. How, under such circumstances, does one respond to one's obligation to preach the gospel, and how can we hope that men and women may become effectively and experientially alerted to the living meaning and truth which must lie behind and beyond the investigations which I have been pursuing in these lectures, if there is any truth in them?

I have thought it necessary to add a postscript to the lectures about this question of the apprehension of truth because I dared to hope as I wrote them that they might engage with this matter of truth and the gospel as they are to be looked for, responded to and lived out. But as I delivered them I felt more and more that they were but the most preliminary survey of ground which had yet to be entered upon and lived in. I suppose it is the inevitable lot of anyone who believes himself to have an inescapable call to attempt to speak of the realities of God and man, to know always that he finishes rather far short of the point at which he ought really to begin. But this necessary reminder of the distance one is from apprehending and conveying that truth which seems none the less in some way to have got hold of one, served also to direct my attention to the essential rôle in the practice of the living discovery of truth of the community.

In these lectures on God and man in Jesus Christ I have found practically no space for any reference to, and certainly no opportunity for any discussion of, the communal dimension of personality and the fulfilment of personalness or of the communal dimension of Christian living and of the apprehension of the truth of the things concerning Jesus. I wish to register this here for two reasons, both connected with types of 'follow-up' which the experiment of these lectures would require if they are to lead in the direction of the practical apprehension and application of truth. That is, if we are to validly engage in an 'argument for the truth of Christianity'.

The first reason is that I do not believe that it is arguments and investigations of the type exemplified in these lectures which play the primary rôle either in persuading people to pay attention to the question 'What is truly involved in believing in Jesus Christ?' (see Preface, pp. vi f.) or in helping people to work out an answer to that question. People will be persuaded to take up this question only in so far as they come across groups of persons who are attempting to be believers in Jesus Christ and who are displaying a style of life and a manner of involvement in practical realities which are *prima facie* authentic, i.e. have something about them which invite further attention. On matters of fundamental importance, persons must gain a hearing for arguments. Christians, therefore, cannot hope to regain evangelistic effectiveness simply by renovating the terms or the types of their argument. We have to demonstrate authentic practice before we can hope for effective preaching. And this is entirely in the logic of the things concerning Jesus. Jesus was discovered to be the Word of God and the Logos of the cosmos in and through his personal embodied living. God makes himself known in human practice. Those who believe that it is in the following of Jesus that God is above all to be known and shown can scarcely expect to find any other effective way of learning for themselves or of gaining a hearing from others than the way of involvement and practice. So it is also that the meaning and truth of the arguments deployed in these lectures can only be discovered by those who are already sympathetic to the question about Jesus in so far as they are willing to throw in their lot with others in the practical pursuit of the human, the worshipful and the Christ-like in and in relation to that materiality and historicity with which they are individually and corporately involved. Thus unless the arguments of these lectures can be followed up by and tied in with corporate and individual experiments in attempted Christian practice, they can lead nowhere.

Secondly, I wish to draw attention to the bearing of this dimension of community on my other main question 'What is really involved in being a man?' (Preface, p. vii). Any serious answer to this question must clearly include consideration of that actual community which shapes a man and that to-be-hoped-for and striven-for community which enables that fulfilment of a man which interlocks with and contributes to the fulfilment of other men. Personalness has a communal dimension, and individuality neither emerges from, nor is to be fulfilled by, isolation. Hence the investigations of these lectures need to be followed up in relation to the social side of the life of men, and the things concerning Jesus need to be carefully scrutinized in relation to all those ways in which human togetherness is threatened, fails or never begins to be developed. We shall not be able to make satisfactory and effective sense of the cosmic significance of Jesus unless and until we develop and re-develop practical implications of the social significance of Jesus. The Kingdom of God stands for the fulfilment of the personal purposes of the universe in a perfected and a perfecting society. I do not myself see effective sense being made of the theological and anthropological realities of the things concerning Jesus without commitment to the social and political dimensions of men's living. Thus it becomes clearer than ever that the effective and life-enhancing things about the truth as it is in Jesus have been scarcely touched on in the lectures which might, at best, turn out to be a sort of intellectual girding up of the loins for a task which makes demands of the will and the emotions quite as much as of the intellect.

Theologically speaking, too, I have not only failed to move on to effective territory concerned with working out the truth about man. I have scarcely moved either into any effective discussion of the mystery of God. I have made no reference to or discussion of that articulation of the understanding of the mystery of God which emerges from the things concerning Jesus and which is symbolized by the doctrine of the Trinity. Such a discussion is very necessary if one is to follow up the present set of investigations in any effective way. For although the doctrine of the Trinity has been much theorized about and obscured by many theories it is, in essence, a non-theoretical distillation and articulation of the experience of the God and Father of Jesus Christ which came to men as they responded to the things concerning Jesus in the power of the continuing presence of his Spirit. As such, the doctrine of the Trinity points to many avenues of investigation which can throw some light on the reality of the transcendentally personal God in his relations with the derived personalities whose ultimate hope and fulfilment he is. In particular, I am sure that the reality to which the symbol of the Trinity points is highly relevant to that balance of the individual, the relational and the communal in which the fulfilment of personalness may be looked for.

Thus, if these lectures have any value or significance it will be only as they are a preface and pointer to a continuing programme of investigation and commitment. The end of the argument in which these lectures join will come, I believe, only when we are brought to that perfected community which is the fulfilment of humanness through Jesus Christ in the reality of God himself. Only then may we hope to know for certain both what the truth truly is and that such truth truly exists. Meanwhile, I suggest that in living by faith we are, in fact, arguing for and searching for truth. The peculiar nature of the faith which is response to the reality in Jesus Christ is the assurance that the truth for which we seek has already sought and found us. The peculiar danger of faith is to pervert this assurance into a self-centred conviction that we have found the truth. So we can seek because we have been found and are ourselves committed to putting whatever we find at the service of and to the test of further seeking. This is the experiment which is living .And I suspect that what the argument of these lectures comes to is the case for maintaining that the only experiment which gives room enough for truly human living is the experiment into God. Further, this is the experiment which is both possible and has every hope of a successful outcome because a proper understanding of the things concerning Jesus gives us reason to believe that God has undertaken the experiment of being a man.

POSTSCRIPT NOTE

Since the publication of these Bampton Lectures, I have taken up the discussion of the doctrine of the Trinity in *The Contradiction of Christianity* (especially chapter 10), SCM Press 1976.

THE LORD'S PRAYER

C. F. EVANS

SCM PRESS LTD

0 334 02715 2

First published in 1963 by SPCK

This edition published 1997 by
SCM Press Ltd
9-17 St Albans Place, London N1 0NX

Printed in Great Britain by
Biddles Ltd, Guildford and King's Lynn

Contents

v

Foreword by John Bowden

The immediate cause of this reissue is sufficiently interesting to be worth mentioning. I had been invited to preach a sermon at Mattins in Thorley Church, on the Isle of Wight, and the New Testament reading contained the Lukan Version of the Lord's Prayer. Knowing the congregation a bit, I thought that they would enjoy a detective-story-like sermon on the different versions of the Lord's Prayer and its subsequent history, illustrating the way in which prayer is never static but undergoes a living process of growth, even in this, the most famous of all Christian prayers.

To make sure I had got my facts right, on the train on the way down I read Christopher Evans' little book on the Lord's Prayer, which I had bought when it first came out in 1963. (It had been delivered as the Lenten course in Durham Cathedral the previous year and was published, with some additional notes, by SPCK.) I had not read it for a long time, and I had forgotten just what a masterpiece it was. And the congregation much enjoyed the sermon.

A couple of weeks later I was in Oxford talking with an old friend, Robert Morgan, who teaches New Testament there. Out of the blue he suddenly remarked, 'Have you ever considered a reissue of Christopher Evans' marvellous little book on the Lord's Prayer?' So I wrote to a somewhat surprised Christopher Evans to make sure that it was possible, and here it is. Christopher Evans feels somewhat apologetic about the old-fashioned non-inclusive language which he used—but everyone else used it at that time, and it's quite impracticable to change it. He has added an additional note on more recent views about Jesus' use of the word 'Abba', along with a bibliography.

Christopher Evans was my teacher at Oxford and the man who introduced me to the New Testament; he was also a very good college chaplain indeed and more than anyone else helped to shape my spirituality. It therefore gives us at SCM Press great pleasure to make this book available once again. But quite apart from my personal feelings, it also has to be said that it just is an excellent book!

July 1997

1

The Form of the Prayer

THE earliest known commentary on the Lord's Prayer,
that of the African theologian Tertullian (c. 160–230),
says of it that it embraces "as it were the whole of the
Lord's discourse, the whole record of his instruction: so
that without exaggeration there is comprised in the
prayer an epitome of the entire gospel".[1] This cannot
be said without exaggeration, to which, indeed, Tertullian was much inclined. There are features which would
have to have a place in any epitome of the Gospel which
do not appear in the Prayer, such as the saving death of
Christ and his resurrection, the Son of Man and his
coming, the Holy Spirit, and perhaps more besides. But
for all his exaggeration it is clear what Tertullian means.
He is alluding to the succinctness of the Prayer, to its
extreme brevity, of which he further says that it nevertheless "rests upon the foundation of a great and fruitful
interpretation, and in proportion as it is restrained in
wording, so it is copious in meaning".[2] His words are
borne out by experience. Careful study of some aspect of
the life and teaching of Jesus will often lead back to a
clause in the Lord's Prayer, where it will be found sum-
marized in terse form, while careful study of a clause in
the Prayer will certainly lead out far and wide over the
range of that life and teaching to explain it. Hence, each

generation is likely to find reflected in its understanding of the Prayer much of its understanding of the Gospel as a whole, and also its own particular problems in understanding that Gospel. The understanding and the problems will be discovered to go closely together.

The first problem for us, as it has not been for some previous ages, lies in the form and wording of the Prayer, and a consideration of this problem will be seen to take us step by step a longer way that we might imagine. The Prayer is given us in two places—Matt. 6.9–13 and Luke 11.2–4,[3] but neither the occasion on which it was given, nor the intention with which it was given, nor the text of what is given, are the same. In Matthew the occasion is the Sermon on the Mount, which is being delivered throughout chapters 5–7; in Luke it is in the course of the journey to Jerusalem, when Jesus has been praying alone, and is asked by one of the disciples to teach them to pray as John the Baptist had taught his disciples. In Matthew the intention is to give a pattern for praying—"After this manner pray ye", that is, as the context shows, briefly and succinctly, and not like the heathen who use vain repetitions in the belief that they will be heard by dint of many words.[4] The intention in Luke is to provide a model prayer to be used on all Christian occasions: "When[ever] ye pray, say . . .". The text of the Prayer in the Authorized Version is substantially the same in both places, with the exception that in Matthew it ends with a doxology, "For thine is the kingdom, and the power, and the glory, for ever. Amen", which is absent from Luke. This difference of text is reflected in the liturgy of the Church, in which the Prayer is said some-

2

times with, and sometimes without, the doxology.[5] What is the explanation of these differences?

In previous centuries the method of dealing with the somewhat surprising circumstance that we have not one but four accounts of the life and teaching of Jesus, and with the variations and discrepancies between them, has generally been the method of harmonization. It began at least as early as the second century with the Syrian theologian Tatian and his *Diatessaron* (that is, the Gospel "of the four together"), and it has continued until almost yesterday. Such information as was furnished by the gospels of the outlines of Jesus' life and movements was pooled to make a framework, and into this were somehow fitted the events of his life and his teaching. If there were in the gospels two accounts of an event or piece of teaching which were similar but had serious discrepancies, harmonization required that we suppose that two separate events are being narrated, as, for example, that Jesus twice cleansed the Temple, once at the beginning of his ministry,* and again at the end;† or that he gave the same piece of teaching twice in variant forms, as, for example, the Lord's Prayer. The second commentary on the Lord's Prayer to come down to us is that of the Alexandrian theologian Origen (*c.* 185–253), perhaps the first really learned man to be a Christian, and the first great biblical scholar. Origen notes these discrepancies in the case of the Lord's Prayer, and he offers three possible explanations of them. Either Matthew and Luke are describing the same occasion, but the differences, he says, are against this; or they are describing two different

* John 2.13–22.
† Mark 11.15–19 and parallels in Matt. and Luke.

3

occasions, but it is the same prayer which is being given on each occasion; or they are describing two different occasions, and the prayers, though similar in some respects, are two different prayers. He himself seems to favour the last explanation, though he makes no further use of it in his commentary.[6] That is, Origen harmonizes. This method always creaked at the joints, and it never proved really successful in handling the gospels in a convincing way. At times it led to ridiculous results.[7] The critical study of the New Testament in the last hundred years has completely undermined it, and nowadays no scholar would set himself to construct a harmony. He would proceed along different lines, and these lines often open up new vistas which have previously been concealed by harmonization. What lines are these?

The first is textual criticism. The Authorized Version is, so far as the New Testament is concerned, a translation from the Greek. After a thousand years of a Latin Bible in the West enthusiasm at the rediscovery of Greek in general, and of the Greek of the New Testament in particular, was immense. In 1516 the Renaissance scholar Erasmus had printed at Basle a Greek New Testament. The text used was that of a twelfth-century manuscript, except for Revelation, which being missing from this manuscript was supplied from another. This text of Erasmus, subsequently corrected from some sixteen other manuscripts, was later issued in 1550 by Robert Stephanus with all the prestige of the Royal Press in Paris, and it so won its way that it got itself the name of the Textus Receptus, or Received Text. This was the text which was translated into English as the Authorized Version, which thus rests upon the basis of a late single Greek manuscript somewhat revised. How far can this be taken as giving us what the authors of the books of the New Testament actually wrote? Since the appearance of the Authorized Version a vast number of manuscripts, not only Greek but also early translations from Greek into Latin, Syriac, Coptic, and other languages have come to light. They cover most centuries as far back as the fourth. A few papyrus texts carry us back to the third century.

All this, along with quotations from the New Testament made by the Christian fathers, which give us the form of the text as they knew it, provide the textual critic with the material on which he gets to work. His object is to attempt to reach back through the corruptions, to which all texts are subject through human fallibility in copying, to what the authors originally wrote. His method is highly complicated and technical, but, very briefly, it is first to classify and arrange all this material in groups or families according to their similarities, and then to use them in this classified form to detect, if he can, how this or that difference in wording has arisen as a misunderstanding, or correction, or corruption of another, until he reaches the point where either the earliest and most reliable evidence concurs, in which case he is relatively sure of what the author wrote, or it is equally divided between two possibilities, in which case he has to make a guess at what was the original on some other ground.

By the canons of this textual criticism it is quite certain that the doxology in Matthew's version of the Lord's Prayer is not original. It is not there in the great fourth-century authorities, and appears for the first time in a manuscript of the fifth century, and so passed into later manuscripts, until it reaches us via the twelfth-century manuscript lying behind the Authorized Version.[8] Hence in the Revised Version, which is a revision of the Authorized Version in the light of this textual criticism, the doxology is removed from the text of Matthew and placed in the margin, prefixed by the words, "Many authorities, some ancient, but with variations, add...". At some time and place we can no longer discover, the doxology began to be used. That this had happened comparatively early in at least one part of the Church appears from a rather curious early Christian writing called the *Didache* or "The Teaching of the Twelve Apostles", which is generally placed in Syria, but at dates varying from A.D. 90 to 230, for it contains the Lord's Prayer in Matthew's version with a doxology, though the doxology has a slightly different wording.[9]

The reason for the doxology is not difficult to guess. It was a familiar Jewish form of prayer. It is found in a model prayer of King David: "Thine, O Lord, is the greatness, and the power, and the glory, and the victory, and the majesty ... thine is the kingdom, O Lord",* and it was especially common in Jewish prayers in New Testament times in the form: "Praised be the name of thy glorious kingdom for ever and always." It may be that a Jewish Christian would regard "Deliver us from evil" as an impossibly abrupt ending for a prayer. Probably it was in the use of the prayer in Christian worship that the doxology came naturally to be added—though its earliest occurrence, in the *Didache*, is in the context of the use of the Lord's Prayer in private prayer—and it is found in varying forms in all the great liturgies

* 1 Chron. 29.11.

6

which established themselves in the Church by the fourth century, so passing into the text of Matthew's Gospel. When we use it, therefore, we are not repeating what Jesus said in this connection (though as a Jew he may well have used doxology in prayer), or what Matthew wrote. We are dependent here on Christian tradition as it had grown and expanded, and we are making that tradition our own.

However, what textual criticism gives with one hand it may take away with the other. While it solves one problem by removing a discrepancy between the two versions of the Prayer, at the same time and by the same process it creates other problems by bringing to light even greater discrepancies between them which had hitherto lain hidden. The rest of Matthew's version it leaves as it is in the Authorized Version, but it is able to show that the text of Luke's version according to the Authorized Version is in important respects different from what Luke wrote, and that in the course of time what Luke wrote has been assimilated to what Matthew had written, no doubt because Matthew's version was in any case felt to be better as a prayer, and also because Matthew's Gospel, almost from the time of its appearance, became the favourite gospel in large areas of the Church and the norm for the others. What Luke wrote, as textual criticism is able to recover it, is what is printed in the Revised Version, and what Origen, as is clear from his commentary, had in front of him, namely—

Father
Hallowed be thy name
Thy kingdom come
Give us day by day our daily bread

7

And forgive us our sins; for we ourselves also forgive
    every one that is indebted to us
And bring us not into temptation[10]

There is no surviving evidence for this form ever having
been used in any liturgy of the Church, and we ourselves
have never prayed it in this form.

What is now brought to light is less a single prayer
with only minor textual variations than two substantially
different versions of a prayer. Matthew's version, after an
opening address in two parts, "Our Father: the [Father]
in heaven", is constructed in five couplets, which may be
rendered somewhat literally as follows—

Hallowed thy name: come thy kingdom
Be done thy will: as in heaven so on earth
Our bread for to-day: give us to-day
And forgive us our debts: as we also have forgiven
    our debtors
And lead us not into temptation: but deliver us from
    the evil.

In all the couplets except the third the verbs stand at the
front; the first two couplets are dominated by "thy", the
last three by "us" and "our"; the second and the fourth
correspond in having the second half introduced by "as";
only the third runs straight through.[11] It is claimed that
when turned back into Aramaic this gives a sequence of
five couplets, each in two halves, and each half with two
accented stresses, which is said to be a familiar Old
Testament metre.[12] Matthew's version would thus be
poetry, and one scholar refers to Luke's version as a
mutilated version in comparison with it.[13] Another
scholar, on the other hand, can maintain that Luke's
version is not simply a torso, but that when put back into

8

Aramaic it also exhibits a well-known, though different, rhythmical structure—after the single address, "Father", it has seven lines of seven syllables each.[14] Textual criticism thus lays bare two distinct versions, each perhaps with its own poetic form. What is the explanation of this?

Textual criticism prepares the way for what is known as source criticism and form criticism. The first attempts to discover what written sources an evangelist had to hand when he set out to compose his gospel. The second attempts to detect, through observing the shapes of the stories and sayings in the gospels, something of the life they have lived and the use to which they were put in the Church in the early days, when as yet there was no writing, but all was the spoken word. The source critic has deduced from the very close agreement between Matthew and Luke in some passages which are not to be found in Mark, that they had in common a further written source besides Mark, and sometimes the Lord's Prayer has been assigned to this source. The differences between the two versions would then be attributed to the editorial work of one or the other evangelist. Perhaps the more Jewish Matthew added the more Jewish "our" and "in heaven" to the simple "Father", and perhaps expanded the petitions with "thy will be done on earth as in heaven" and with "deliver us from evil". Or perhaps the hellenist Luke abbreviated by pruning away some things that were more specifically Jewish.[15] But if both versions are shown to be poems in their own right, each with its own distinctive structure and rhythm, it becomes more difficult to account for them in this way, and to account for the differences between them as variations of a common version in a written source. For it is unlikely that alterations here and there to a poem will produce another poem. Hence the form critic will be inclined to suppose that the two versions came to Matthew and Luke independently of any written source, that each came along its own line of spoken tradition, perhaps through its use in the particular church to which each evangelist belonged. In its use in the church each will have developed its own rhythmic pattern. Matthew will then have placed his version where it seemed to him most fitting—in that section of his gospel where he has gathered together Jesus' comments on the Jewish duties of religion, almsgiving, prayer, and fasting, as part of that collection of the teachings of Jesus, the Sermon on the Mount, which Matthew has constructed as the new Christian law given on a new holy mount. Luke, who by special touches in his gospel goes out of his way to depict Jesus as a man of prayer,* and who had already shown his interest in the prayers of the Baptist's disciples,† will have introduced it into his story by a picture of Jesus praying alone, and the request of a disciple to be taught to pray as John's disciples had been taught by their master. In this way Luke wishes to trace the prayer which had already been in use in the Church back to its origin in Jesus, the man of prayer.

If this is anything like a correct account of the matter, it follows that we do not know for certain when, and in what circumstances, Jesus gave the prayer, and we may not have in either version the exact wording in which he gave it. Each version has a history of growth behind it,

* E.g. Luke 3.21; 6.12; 9.18, 28, all of which are added by Luke to his sources.[3]

† Luke 5.33, added by Luke in taking over Mark.

as it has been put to use in the worship of the Church before any gospels were written, and when it reaches the evangelists it does so in a form which owes something to the spiritual experience of those Christian communities which have been praying it for some years.

In this the Lord's Prayer is not peculiar to the gospels, but is rather characteristic of them. To take an instance which is as important as that of the Lord's Prayer, the institution of the Eucharist at the Last Supper. In the Authorized Version the accounts of Matthew, Mark, and Luke are in close agreement.* There is a breaking of the bread with the words interpreting it: "This is my body" (in Luke, "which is given for you; this do in remembrance of me"), followed by the blessing of the cup and the words connecting it with the sacrificial death of Jesus: "This is my blood of the new testament, which is shed for many" (in Matthew, "for the forgiveness of sins"; Luke, "This cup is the new testament in my blood, which is shed for you"); and then in Mark and Matthew, but not in Luke, the vow of Jesus not to drink henceforth of the fruit of the vine until he drinks it new in the kingdom of God. So far we have substantially the same account with some variations. The only big difference is that in Luke this is all preceded by another cup which Jesus takes and blesses with the words: "Take this and divide it among yourselves: For I say unto you that I will not drink of the fruit of the vine, until the kingdom of God shall come." But here also textual criticism comes in to disturb an apparent harmony, for a number of important manuscripts omit from Luke's account all words accompanying the giving of the bread after "This is my body", and the

* Mark 14.22-5; Matt. 26.26-9; Luke 22.14-20.

11

whole account of the cup which follows, together with its sacrificial words.* Many scholars, perhaps the majority, consider that this shorter text is what Luke wrote, and that his version has been later assimilated to that of the others or to that of Paul in 1 Cor. 11. Although the makers of the Revised Version were not sure enough to print this shorter version as Luke's text and only placed it in the margin as a possibility, the makers of the New English Bible have no such hesitation. The effect of this is that we have in Luke's text not bread followed by cup but cup followed by bread,[16] and further that we have no words with the cup giving it a sacrificial meaning.

The possibility now opens up that there was not one fixed and established account in the Church of the institution of the sacrament, but at least two, and that they were different—the one, bread and cup, and the cup a memorial of the Lord's death, and the other, cup and bread, with both thought of as a foretaste of the banquet of the coming kingdom of God.[17] And the further possibility arises that, as with the Lord's Prayer, both accounts have been handed down, not simply in the interests of preserving a historical reminiscence of something Jesus had once done and said, but as components of the worship of Christian communities in which they were being used week by week as a living and growing tradition, and that something of how those communities came to experience the sacrament spiritually is now woven into the accounts. We may not know exactly and verbatim what Jesus did and said, because we now have it refracted through the experience of those who, by using what he did and said, had come to apprehend more of what he was to them.

* I.e. Luke 22. 19bf.

Or again, we have in Matthew and Luke a parable of the lost sheep.* It is evidently the same story—a man has a hundred sheep, one of which strays, and the man leaves the rest and searches until he finds it, and there is more joy over finding it than over the rest. But, as in the case of the Lord's Prayer, neither the occasion, nor the intention, nor the text are the same in the two accounts. The occasion in Matthew's Gospel is an instruction by Jesus of his disciples on how they should treat one another in the Church, and the intention matches the occasion, which is to teach them that "it is not the will of your Father that one of these little ones should perish". The occasion in Luke is an objection by Pharisees and scribes to Jesus' consorting with publicans and sinners, and again the intention matches this particular occasion, which is to teach that "there is more joy in heaven over one sinner that repenteth, than over ninety and nine righteous persons, which need no repentance". Sometimes this parable has also been assigned to the written source which Matthew and Luke are said to have had in common, but again the differences in telling what is the same story suggest that the parable came to each evangelist along a separate path, and that along that path it had received different adaptations. It is surely significant that the purpose to which the parable is put in Matthew's Gospel fits so well with what is a strong feature of that gospel as a whole, namely, its concern with the Church and its discipline, and that the use to which it is put in Luke's Gospel fits so well with what is a strong feature of that gospel, namely the compassion of Jesus for sinners. It is difficult to resist the conclusion, once we have given up harmonizing, that the parable has had a history and a

* Matt. 18.12ff; Luke 15.3–7.

13

development in different parts of the Church, and that in that development it has been moulded by what men wished to say through it in the light of their Christian experience.

These instances are only one or two, but a great deal of the gospels is open to this kind of analysis, and from it a general principle emerges. When we are listening to the words of Jesus in the gospels there are generally two voices to be heard. There is the voice of Jesus—rabbi, prophet, messiah—speaking in Galilee or Jerusalem in the situation which confronted him there, and there is a voice in a Christian community somewhere—Antioch, Corinth, Ephesus, Rome, Jerusalem—speaking years later in the situation in which Christians now lived, but speaking in that situation not simply with their own words, but through Jesus' words, because those words are never for them the words of a dead rabbi, prophet, or messiah, but the words of him who is their living Lord, and who, because he is what he is, speaks to all situations.

Sometimes we may think that we can in some measure distinguish the two voices; sometimes, as for example in the Fourth Gospel, the two voices are so blended that they cannot any longer be heard apart. This is not something to be regretted, for Jesus himself appears to be responsible for it. He himself wrote nothing, and gave no instructions, so far as we know, about writing, or even about the preservation of his words. They do not come to us tape-recorded. With what we can only judge to be a sort of divine recklessness they were committed to his disciples, for a future time which he left largely unspecified, and they were taken over and interpreted for the disciples by a Holy Spirit about whom he had said hardly anything at all.[18] This may tell us something about the method by which God has chosen to reveal himself and his truth to us.

The method is that of incarnation, but incarnation would seem to mean more than that God unites himself with human nature and human conditions simply in the figure of Jesus for his lifetime, the union to be dissolved so far as we are concerned once that life is over. God has also committed himself to our human nature and human conditions in what men do with the words and deeds of Jesus as they receive them for their salvation, and as they use them as the guide of their lives. What we have in the gospels is the result of this union—not the naked words of Jesus, but those words as they have become through the work they have done in men. There would seem to be no way back to a confident use of the gospels for our spiritual illumination, guidance, and nourishment, unless this truth is boldly grasped. The necessity of grasping it appears from the fact that even the simplest and most repeated act of the Christian, the recitation of the Lord's Prayer, cannot now be just a repetition of what Jesus once taught, precisely in the words in which he taught it, but only the recitation of what has resulted from the inter-penetration of the words of Jesus with the minds and spirits of his first disciples.

2

Holy Father

Is the Lord's Prayer original and unique? Some form of belief in the uniqueness of Jesus is inseparable from Christianity itself. If all sense of the originality of Jesus disappeared, Christianity itself would disappear with it. What, however, would we be supposed to mean by uniqueness or originality in this connection? The word "unique" has almost lost any precise meaning in English, being now used as a loose synonym for "remarkable". Its proper meaning is "the only one of its kind", as was, so the ancients supposed, the phoenix, which rose again out of its own ashes. Similarly "original" now means "striking" or "novel", whereas its original meaning was "not derived or dependent". The first Christians certainly believed Jesus to be unique in the strict sense of the word. He was the only one of his kind. That was their gospel. What they considered unique, however, was not in the first place his teaching but his person, and that by which his person was grasped, which also was not in the first place his teaching but his death and resurrection. This uniqueness was expressed by speaking of him as Christ or Lord, or as the bearer of the name which is above every name, or by speaking of his death as the sacrifice which fulfils all that was intended by sacrifices and annuls them, or of his resurrection as the first instalment of the general resurrection, the beginning of the end of the world. Nevertheless, they did preserve his teaching, handing it down in various connections and for various purposes until it attained a fixed form in writing, and presumably in doing so they did not find that teaching incompatible with the uniqueness which they had already claimed for him on other grounds, but rather of one piece with it.

But in what sense is the teaching of Jesus unique? If we meant by the uniqueness and originality of his teaching that it was remarkable and novel, we should indeed be saying something, e.g. that it would find a place in any collection made from the world's great religious teachers, but that would not be a Christian judgement, and a Christian would be comparatively bored by it. If we meant that it is unique and original in the strict sense, then the difficulty is that the critical scholar proceeds, and must proceed, as if it were not the only one of its kind, and he sets out to reduce the originality by placing it on its background, adducing parallels, and showing its dependence on what has gone before. The more parallels he can adduce the better pleased he is, and he welcomes discoveries like the Dead Sea Scrolls because they fill in some of the hitherto unknown background. Indeed, can teaching ever be unique in the strict sense? Would it not be unintelligible to the hearers if it did not make close contact with what was already in their minds? This question of the relation between the new and the old in the teaching of Jesus is raised by the opening address of the Lord's Prayer and the first petition which goes with it.

Some form of address to God or gods as "father" would appear to be as old and widespread as religion, as mankind itself. Except in the rare matriarchal societies, or where the state has assumed to itself the parental functions, the natural fact of fatherhood has impressed itself deeply as a dominant in human life, and has supplied a basic image for conceiving the relation between God and man. This is so in primitive societies and in the dawning civilizations of Assyria and Babylon. Over the Greek pantheon of gods Zeus was established in a supreme position as "Father of gods and men", and the Latin equivalent to him, Jupiter, is simply $Z\hat{\epsilon}v \pi\acute{\alpha}\tau\epsilon\rho$, "O Father Zeus". [1] Father, however, is a comprehensive word, and behind any use of it in religion and prayer will lie some particular understanding of what constitutes fatherhood, or some particular aspect of it, which is being pressed to supply an analogy of the relation of God and man. The depth and adequacy of the religion will depend on this understanding, or on the aspect chosen and the way it is applied.

The Christian will be chiefly concerned with what happened to the word in the Hebrew, as the immediate preparation for the Christian, religion. It does not seem to have belonged in that religion from the outset, but to have been received into it at a later stage, to stand alongside other ways of speaking about God, and it never captures the field or becomes a fixed and prevailing image. This may account for its comparative rarity in the Old Testament (God is not once addressed as "father" in the Psalms), [2] and for the reserve with which it is used. It is purified and disciplined by being brought into connection with the idea of the covenant bond between God and his people, and with the Hebrew understanding of the family, and of the rôle of the father in the family.

In this purification the first thing to go is precisely what must stand first in any dictionary definition of the word "father", and what in other religions strongly coloured the picture of God's relation to men, that is, the male parent, who is such by physically begetting a child. So characteristic of heathenism was this thought to be that only very rarely in the Old Testament is God said to be the father of Israel by virtue of having begotten or created Israel.* The thought of begetting survives chiefly in the metaphorical sense that a man's character is revealed in what he produces, as when the devil is called "the father of lies" because lies are his natural product, or that a man's actions betray his origins, as when a peaceful man is called a "son of peace".† Room is thus made in the word for what is social and ethical in place of what is physical. In the Hebrew social pattern, with its strong sense of the family, which is often called "a father's house", [3] the position of the father was expressed by lordship. He was the possessor and master, the ruling will and guardian of the right, the centre from which the life of the family flowed—the Hebrew version of the Latin *patria potestas*. Love and care are suggested, even presumed, in the word "father", but they are not what the word is used principally to assert. The correlative of "father" is not so much "child" as "son". A man living as a father is one who wills to reproduce a certain character in a son, and who governs and disciplines him to that end. A son is such because he obeys the will of a father and reproduces a father's character. Hence the language of father and son is more often used of the proper attitude of the son to the father than of the father to the son. [4] All this is transferred to the relationship between God and Israel. God in the Old Testament is not the father of all men by virtue of having

* Mal. 2.10; Deut. 32.18; Isa. 45.11.   † John 8.44; Luke 10.6.

created them, but the father of his people Israel by virtue of his choice, deliverance, instruction, and discipline of them. The son of God is Israel as a single whole; occasionally, at a later date, it is individual Israelites, but even then only as members of that whole.* The last two centuries before Christ saw the growth of a piety deeply grounded in this conception, and in this period the phrase, "Our [my, your, his] Father in heaven", is found regularly in the language of the rabbis, and, without "in heaven", in Jewish prayers, notably in the classical Jewish prayer, the *Shemōneh Esrēh* or *Eighteen Benedictions*. [5]

Against this background is the teaching of Jesus about the fatherhood of God old or new or both? The question is not easy to answer, because, in the first place, the evidence is uncertain. If the Synoptic Gospels are taken as they stand, God is there, as in Judaism, the father of a family, which is also a people standing in a covenant relationship with him, reciprocating his fatherhood with sonship, which is their obedience to his will as it has been made known; only now it is the disciples of Jesus, knowing the will of God as it has been supremely declared by Jesus, who are the family, and who are the people with whom God makes the new covenant. [6] Love and affection are contained in the word. The Father who governs the world with providential care will supply the good things which the disciples need.† But principally God as Father is the supreme authority,‡ who holds in his hands the

* Ex. 4.22; Hos. 11.1 for the first (cf. also Isa. 1.2; 63.16; Jer. 3.22; 31.9, 20; Ps. 82.6); Ecclus. 4.10; Wisd. 2.13 for the second.

† Matt. 7.11=Luke 11.13; Matt. 6.25-33=Luke 12.22-31.

‡ Matt. 11.27=Luke 10.22; Matt. 23.9; Mark 13.32; 14.36; Luke 23.46.

final things,* who reveals his own truth,† sustains his own purposes,‡ the righteous judge towards whom all human actions are to be directed as to the only one whose judgement is finally valid.§ It is in reproducing his perfection‖ and his charity which knows no bounds¶ that the disciples become his sons.

However, the possibility has to be reckoned with that this aspect of Jesus' teaching has been considerably augmented and developed as it was handed down in the life of the Church and in the light of Christian experience. Thus, at one end of the scale, there are in Mark's Gospel only three references to God as Father in the teaching of Jesus—one in the prayer of Jesus himself in Gethsemane, one in the absolute form "the Father" as a metonym for God, and only one, and that doubtful, in relation to the disciples. 7 At the other end of the scale there are just over a hundred references in John's Gospel, but only one of them refers to God as the Father of the disciples** and the rest are of a special kind. God is either the Father of Jesus, or "the Father" simply. This absolute and more abstract use is rare both in Judaism and in the Synoptic Gospels, but along with its correlate, "the Son", used of Jesus, it dominates the Gospel and First Epistle of John, and would seem to be less the teaching of Jesus himself than a precipitate in the Christian mind of the Incarnation. The teaching about God's fatherhood in relation to men is found largely in Matthew's Gospel, and it is generally

* Matt. 10.32f; 15.13; 20.23; 25.34; Luke 24.49.
† Matt. 11.25f=Luke 10.21; Matt. 16.17.
‡ Matt. 11.26; 18.10–14; Luke 12.32; 22.29.
§ Matt. 6.1–8,16–18; 18.35.   ‖ Matt. 5.48=Luke 6.36.
¶ Matt. 5.44f=Luke 6.35.   ** John 20.17.

agreed that Matthew is particularly concerned to build up the divine fatherhood and the sonship of the disciples into a major theme. He can be observed introducing to this end a favourite phrase "my [your] Father in heaven", which already belonged to Jewish piety, and which is confined to his among the gospels. Thus "Our Father, the [Father] in heaven" at the beginning of his version of the Lord's Prayer may be due to him, or to the milieu which he represented. On the other hand it cannot be ruled out that on occasion Luke may have changed an original "Father" into "God".[8] These differences in the gospel traditions make it difficult to discern how exactly the matter lies, but the evidence points to Jesus having been more reserved in his teaching about the divine fatherhood than the gospels now allow it to appear. There is, however, reason to believe that Jesus may have been distinctive, not in multiplying the use of the word "Father" but in intensifying it.

Mark, who has so little about God's fatherhood in his account of the teaching of Jesus, nevertheless records that in the critical moment of his prayer in Gethsemane Jesus addressed God with the words "Abba, Father", and twice in his epistles Paul speaks of Christians as so possessed by the spirit of Jesus' own sonship that they also "cried out", either in prayer or in the confession of their faith (at baptism?), "Abba, Father".[9] This is very curious. Why should two words for the same thing, one Aramaic (Abba, left untranslated in our English versions) and the other Greek (δ $\pi\alpha\tau\dot{\eta}\rho$ translated "Father" in our versions), be left standing side by side? Why not use either the one or the other? There may be something special, even unique, here. The word "abba" is Aramaic, the vernacular which

22

Jesus spoke. Further, it is a diminutive, belonging to the vocabulary of children, like the Greek πάππα and our "papa". It was a secular word of daily life, the intimate and familiar address of the child to its earthly father, and Dr J. Jeremias can declare that in the whole field of Jewish literature he cannot find another instance of its use as an address to God. Always there it is "my father", "our father", "our father in heaven".[10] If this is so, it will have impressed itself upon the first Christians as an extraordinarily bold and intimate form of address to God, betokening first a unique relation of Jesus himself to God, and then a like relation to God into which they had been admitted through him. It will have left its traces, as the two occurrences in Paul's epistles show, after the Church had ceased to speak Aramaic, and it may lie behind other instances of "Father" in the gospels, perhaps, for example, behind the opening word of Luke's version of the Lord's Prayer.

This very intensification of one aspect of fatherhood in the word "abba" raises in a particularly acute form a problem which attaches to all our language about God, and which is therefore felt especially in prayer. It is that no image or analogy can be taken as it stands as adequate to its task of speaking about God. There has to take place what has been called a "stripping of the images" if analogies are not to be overworked, and to be pressed for more than they are entitled to give, and the word "father", for all its intimacy and the sanction which Jesus has given it, is not exempt. Already in the Old Testament it had been stripped of its most immediate connotation, that of physical begetting, but the process cannot be arrested at this point. If it were, "abba" might be responsible for ensconcing at the very heart of religion a permanent infantilism. It is not uncommon to hear the practice of prayer itself based on the analogy that, as an earthly father loves to hear his child prattling to him of its needs, so it is between God and us. This is disastrous. It leads to the suspicion that prayer belongs only to our childhood or to the childhood of the race, and it is always open to the riposte that normally children are expected to grow up, and that there is something gravely wrong with them if they do not.[11] The New Testament itself contains some very severe condemnations of perpetual immaturity.*

It is, therefore, necessary to repeat that in the Bible the correlative of "father" is not so much "child" as "son", that is, the one who does the father's will and reproduces his character. But the image cannot come to rest even at this point. "In modern European thought a growing son who in every action remained totally dependent on his father is unthinkable."[12] When, therefore, the Fourth Gospel represents precisely such a constant and total dependence of a son upon a father as the very inner secret of the nature and work of Christ, it does so in order to state that the creation and the redemption of the world have their source in an initiative within the Godhead, which is met by a perfect response also within the Godhead, and it can only do so if something of what is ordinarily meant by "son" is thought away in the process. This particular Son is not one who grows up, or needs to grow up; unlike any human son he is the equal and *alter ego* of his Father, and what is meant by calling him Son is that his life on earth is response, and that the response is unbroken and perfect. It was for this reason that later

* 1 Cor. 3.1ff; Heb. 5.11–14.

24

Christian theology, in reflecting on the New Testament truths, felt bound to reintroduce precisely that aspect of fatherhood, physical begetting, which the Old Testament had previously expelled as heathen. This could now be done without danger of heathenism, since it was to define, not a physical relation of God to the world, but a non-physical relation within the Godhead. Christ is now described in creeds as "the only-begotten Son of the Father", and such a description isolates the essence of his sonship as a perfect communion and response, in which there is no longer any trace of the subordination and inferiority which are naturally suggested by the word "son". The image has been further stripped by the impact of what is revealed of God through Christ. We can thus see how important it is that in the Lord's Prayer the intimate address "Father" is immediately followed by the first of the petitions, "Hallowed be thy name".

It has been suggested that this is not a petition but an affirmation, like the familiar "Blessed be he" which the pious Jew added after the mention of God, but it is probably better taken as the first of the petitions. In all the petitions of the Prayer, with the exception of that for bread, the verb stands first and takes the weight—"be hallowed thy name", "come thy kingdom", "be done thy will", "forgive", "lead not", "deliver". Further, with the exception of the prayer for bread in Luke's version, these verbs are in the aorist tense, which expresses, not a continuous or repeated action, but a point action, a once for all action. "As in the Lord's Prayer, so in the ancient Greek liturgies, the aorist imperative is almost exclusively used. It is the true tense for 'instant' prayer."[13] That is, the Prayer does not contemplate years stretching ahead, or a slow development, or a gradual approximation, or any of the things which are natural to our way of thinking; it demands an immediate fulfilment of what it asks. Moreover, in the first petition, and in Matthew's third, the verb is in the passive, and this passive, like the intransitive in the second petition, represents in Greek a Hebrew turn of speech, whereby the direct mention of God as the subject of an active verb is avoided for reasons of reverence. The sense then is, "Do thou hallow thy name", "Do thou cause thy kingdom to come", "Do thou cause thy will to be done". That is, the Prayer does not envisage human co-operation or the assistance of men as God's agents for getting his work done; it appeals directly to God to accomplish his own work which only he can do.[14]

The first petition is remarkable, and illustrates further how delicate is the question of the relation of the teaching of Jesus to what had gone before. For, while the Name of God is a very common Old Testament concept, and the hallowing of the Name such a frequent expression of Jewish piety as almost to be the Jewish equivalent of our word "religion", we would have to conclude, were it not for this petition in the Prayer, that neither had any place in the mind of Jesus, since neither is mentioned again in the Synoptic Gospels.[15] Behind the concept of the Name of God lies the conjunction of two beliefs. The first is the belief, of which the Old Testament furnishes many instances, that a name is more than a chance appellation by which a person or thing is to be identified. The name distinguishes and expresses the nature and essence of its bearer, and can even be a substitute for what is named. Thus, "for my name's sake" is simply another way of

26

saying "for my sake", and when it is said that God causes his name to dwell in a place, what is meant is that he himself dwells there. The second is the primitive, and originally magical, belief that the name of a god has power, and that to know his name is to be in a position to bring that power to one's aid. This primitive idea also undergoes purification in Hebrew religion, and what purifies it, as it purifies everything it touches, is hallowing or holiness.

Of all the words employed in religious speech "holy" is at once the most difficult to grasp and the most indispensable. It is the most difficult to grasp because, while all other words in religion—father, son, king, righteous, merciful, etc.—are drawn from familiar human experience, and are applied by analogy to God, this is the one word, apart from the word "God" itself, which is not. While other words mark some measure of similarity between God and the world, this word marks the difference between God and all that is not God. Its root meaning appears to have been "separate", "distinct", "other".[16] It denotes, as no other, the supernatural, the transcendent, not in the sense of the spatially remote, but in the sense of what is other than what we are and know. God's holiness is "an equivalent for his deity; and however strong the connotation of moral perfection came to be, this never became, as it is for us, the denotation of the word".[17] Holiness means the God-ness of God, and in Hebrew religion can be predicated of Jehovah alone. To say that God is holy is to say that he is God. To say that things or persons are holy is to say that they have been separated by God to his special possession, and have passed from the sphere of the worldly and familiar into the sphere of the sacred. The Holy One is *sui generis*; there is no analogy of him. For this reason it is the most indispensable word in religion, for it marks the fact that all the other words, which are taken from human experience to be used as analogies, do not fit the God to whom they are applied. If he is Father he is Holy Father, the Father with an almighty difference. The word thus governs the use of all other words in their application to God. It strips the images, and stands guard against their improper use.

The Holy Name is thus God's Name, and this is God himself. The hallowing of the Name means the making of the Name holy, means causing God to be acknowledged for the God he is. This has been called "the most characteristic feature of Jewish ethics both as principle and as motive".[18] It was the heart of the Jewish religion that God's people shall so act, if necessary by martyrdom, that men shall confess the God of Israel to be the one true God. Its opposite was the profanation of the name. But God remains holy, whether men so act or not, and in the Old Testament is said to hallow his own name.* By the appropriate action he brings it about that men are compelled to recognize that he is what he is. The prayer, as in this first petition of the Lord's Prayer, that he will himself hallow his own name, is the prayer that he will so act that all men will own him to be the God he is. It stands at the opening of an ancient Jewish form of prayer, the *Kaddish*: "Magnified and hallowed be his great name in the world which he created according to his will." Standing at the opening of the Lord's Prayer, but found nowhere else in the Synoptic Gospels, it reveals in a sudden flash how deeply and sometimes unexpectedly the teaching of Jesus is grounded in Jewish faith.

* Ezek. 36.22–23; 20.41f; 28.25; 39.27; 38.16.

In these first words of the Prayer, "Abba, Hallowed be thy name", there are juxtaposed with extreme compression nearness and farness, familiarity and distance, likeness and unlikeness, the closest possible analogy and the greatest possible distinction, the simplicity and directness of an intimate earthly approach and awe and reverence before what is totally other. This juxtaposition is the very mainspring of true prayer.[19]

3

Thy kingdom come

Thy will be done, in earth and in heaven

How is the teaching of Jesus to be understood and applied? This is a question raised particularly by the second petition in the Lord's Prayer, "Thy kingdom come", for there is no other single phrase repeated as often in the Synoptic Gospels, and it is found in all the sources and strands into which those gospels may be divided. Mark signals it as supremely the subject of Jesus' preaching when he opens his account of the ministry with the summary statement that Jesus came into Galilee proclaiming the Gospel of God, and saying, "the time is fulfilled, and the kingdom of God is at hand".* After that the phrase is found as the subject matter of parable and prophecy, comment and command.

The transition from the address "Father" to this petition was more natural than our weakened sense of fatherhood allows it to appear. In ancient thought in general, and in Jewish thought in particular, there was no antagonism between "father" and "king" (lord, judge), but rather the closest possible connection. The latter strengthened, and was already contained in, the former, and by union with the concept of God's lordship the father concept was preserved from sentimentality. By his position in the

* Mark 1.15.

30

family the earthly father was also master and judge. This was so of God as father, infrequently as yet in the Old Testament by reason of its comparatively rare use of "father" for God,* but more frequently in later Judaism, especially in prayer, where "our Father, our King" is a regular formula.[1] Thus, the petition that God will hallow his own name, that is, will cause himself to be acknowledged as God, leads naturally in Jewish religion to the prayer that he will actively bring this about, that he will manifest it in action.[2]

In one respect, however, the two petitions are sharply contrasted. The concept of hallowing the name, which is so frequent in the Old Testament and Judaism, is found only in this one place in the Synoptic Gospels, while the phrase "the kingdom of God", which is so frequent in the Synoptic Gospels, is not found as such in the Old Testament at all (though it is found in the sayings of the rabbis). This is not to say that the idea of God's kingdom is not found there. Indeed, a good deal of the Old Testament could be, and has been, brought under the heading "God as King", and this theme is one of the threads which runs through it.[3] Like fatherhood, the rule and authority of the king as constituting a people, and as the source of its life and order, impressed themselves as dominants in human life, only they touched a wider and more public sphere than the family. Like fatherhood, kingship seems not to have belonged to Hebrew religion from the beginning, but to have entered it at a certain stage, and like fatherhood it expressed, and was itself influenced by, the Hebrew understanding of the relation of God and man.[4]

* Mal. 1.6; Ecclus. 23.1,4; 51.10; Tob. 13.4; Wisd. 11.10; 3 Macc. 6.2ff.

God is king, or has made himself king. That, it is generally agreed, is the primary meaning in the Bible of the word rendered "kingdom"—not the place where he rules, but the fact that he rules, his exercise of his rule, his being king. But because this is so, and God's kingship is not an idea, or as we might say an ideal, "kingdom" inevitably has another meaning. God's kingship is exercised somewhere; therefore kingdom comes also to have a second meaning more like our own and closely connected with the first, namely, the sphere where God rules. This in the Old Testament is his people. God's kingdom (rule) is exercised over Israel, and Israel is *his* Kingdom (sphere of rule).*

In time it is seen that this rule is both universal and ever-lasting, as befits God, [5] but again, because this is not an abstract truth or ideal, and is true only as it is shown to be true, a complication arises. God is universal king, and yet he is not, because outside Israel his rule does not run, for it is not acknowledged there. So the hope and demand arise that he must make himself king if he is to be really God. The complication, however, goes deeper. Even in Israel, his kingdom, the people which is the special sphere of his rule, and without which he would not be known for what he is, his rule does not run. His people is a disobedient people. So a deeper and more passionate hope and demand arise, that he will remove the obstacles to his rule in Israel, and the contradictions in human life which obscure it, and that he will establish himself in actuality as king in Israel, and from there over the whole world which is his own. This hope comes to dominate the Jewish faith. There was more than one view of what was involved. Some saw it in more political terms; God would

* 1 Chron. 17.14; 28.5.

32

bring it about that the nation was freed from foreign yoke to become a people devoted to him under his vicegerent, a new David. Others, a great many of the Pharisees for example, saw it more as a spiritual renewal, by which God would bring about a complete devotion to his will as it was expressed in the divine law of Moses and in all that that law implied. Others, who despaired of the world as hopelessly evil and of God's use of human instruments, saw it as God's miraculous transformation of the present order of things and as a new heaven and a new earth. In one way or another Jewish faith came to be orientated towards this hope, and at times to tremble on the brink of its realization. The Jewish rabbis just before or contemporary with Jesus were the first to use the actual phrase "the kingdom of God", or, more usually, in order to avoid from reverence the mention of God, "the kingdom of heaven [the heavens]", as generally in Matthew's Gospel in the New Testament.

Jesus, therefore, did not invent either the phrase or the thought behind it. It lay ready to hand with rich and various suggestions. In his preaching and teaching it is not the subject of lectures or of a sustained exposition, but of a wide variety of types of saying—parable, prophecy, promise, command, warning, threat—and it is not surprising to find it as the subject of one of the two (in Matthew three) petitions in the first half of the Lord's Prayer, which have to do not with human needs but with God's nature and actions in and for themselves. Here is a case where consideration of the teaching of Jesus leads back to a clause in the Prayer and vice-versa. A consideration of that teaching leads to the conclusion that in Jesus' hands the concept of the kingdom of God becomes not only dominant but exceedingly sharp, and in the context of Jewish faith and thought that means that the end of the world note, the note of finality, is increased. What were already present in the conception, a thrust towards a future which is not simply a few more years of time but God's future, and a dissatisfaction so profound that nothing short of a divine resolution of the ambiguities of human life will do, are accentuated. When it is said that Jesus will not drink of the fruit of the vine until he drinks it new in the kingdom of God, or that the apostles shall sit at table eating and drinking in his kingdom which is a kingdom prepared from the foundation of the world, or that many shall come from the east and west and sit at table with the patriarchs, that the rich will hardly enter it, but only those who become as children and whose righteousness exceeds that of the scribes and Pharisees; what is being referred to in terms of the kingdom considered as a sphere to enter is a future state of fulfilment and blessedness which is final and complete.* When it is said that the determined hour has struck and the kingdom of God has drawn near, or that Jesus will not drink of the fruit of the vine until the kingdom of God come, or that certain events will herald its approach, or that some alive will not die before they see it come in power;† what is being referred to in terms of the kingdom considered as God's sovereignty and rule is an order of things which brings history and time as we know them to an end.

This accentuation of the end of the world note can be illustrated by a comparison of the Lord's Prayer with con-

* Mark 14.25; Luke 22.30; Matt. 25.34; 8.11=Luke 13.29; Mark 10.23; Matt. 18.3; 5.20.
† Mark 1.15; Luke 22.18; 21.31; Mark 9.1.

temporary Jewish prayers.[6] The *Eighteen Benedictions* begin, and are primarily occupied, with prayer about the here and now, to which is then attached prayer for the final things in the form of a gathering of the dispersed Israelites, the destruction of their enemies, and the establishment of the Davidic king in a glorified Jerusalem. In all this the kingdom of God is one item.[7] In the Lord's Prayer, on the other hand, all this is reduced to a single petition, unelaborated and unspecified, for the rule of God, and this is placed in the forefront of the prayer as the presupposition of what follows. Whoever prays this prayer is to take his stand at the end of the world, and to pray from that position back into the here and now. This accentuation is further seen in some of the verbs used. On the whole the rabbis spoke of the kingdom being manifested or revealed, and "to take upon oneself the yoke of the kingdom" was an expression for becoming a Jewish proselyte. Characteristic of the gospel vocabulary is the use in connection with the kingdom of the more urgent verbs "come", "come upon", "draw near", which have only remote parallels in the Old Testament. Though "draw near" may be used of movement in space and time, "come" refers primarily to time. Men are not bidden to watch because they do not know the place where the kingdom will appear; in fact they are forbidden to do so.* They are, however, bidden to watch because they do not know, and no one knows except the Father, the moment of its sudden coming.† Time does not simply "like an ever-rolling stream bear all its sons away", it is under the control of God who, having given the world its begin-

---

* Luke 17.20; Matt. 24.26.
† Mark 13.35; Luke 12.35ff; Matt. 24.44–51.

ning, remains its Lord, and will show himself to be God in bringing it to its temporal end which is also its consummation.

A certain contradiction is to be observed here. Sometimes Jesus speaks of the kingdom as a future event, to be watched for, expected, prayed for, and this is clearly so in this petition in the Lord's Prayer.[8] At other times he can speak of it as having drawn so near that men can be held culpable for failing to discern the nature of the time in which they are living, as having arrived in his ministry, even if in hidden form, and as giving that ministry its special character. This has led to a debate amongst the scholars which still continues.[9] Some would say that the first way of speaking is the voice of Jesus, and that the second is the result of later reflections by Christians on the ministry, and their perception of it after the event as indeed the coming of the messiah. Others would say that the voice of Jesus is to be heard in the second way of speaking, and that Christians, unable to hold on to the staggering truth that the kingdom had come with Jesus, lapsed back into the former Jewish habit of hoping for it in the future. The upshot of the debate would seem to be that both ways of speaking are sufficiently rooted in the various strands of the gospels that neither can be finally eliminated at the expense of the other, and that both must be accepted together in spite of the contradiction. Yet is it simply a contradiction and not rather a fruitful tension? To pray "Thy kingdom come" is to take up a position at the end of the world and to pray from there backwards. This kind of prayer is the prayer only of men for whom God really is God, the beginning, middle, and end. The men who are able to pray in this fashion are those who do not despair of God and are not half-hearted, men who have been aroused to the full reality of God, their appetites and desires so whetted that they can now be satisfied with nothing short of God's being all in all. What made the disciples able to pray like this was not any natural powers which they possessed, but precisely the belief engendered in them by Jesus that already in some sense the rule of God was a present fact in his words and deeds, that in his life, however lowly, God was reigning to the full, that the rival power of evil was in retreat before him, and that they stood on the brink of the fulfilment of what their eyes were already seeing.

It is true that a considerable difficulty remains. When the disciples were told to pray "Thy kingdom come" the thought is not of what will happen one fine day or, to use modern and unbiblical language, of "the extension of Christ's kingdom" through the missionary activity of the Church, but of what will come once and for all (that is the force of the aorist imperative), and will come for them, even though the moment of its coming is withheld from their knowledge. This combination of certainty that it will come for them and the withholding of knowledge of the hour of its coming is what gives to their prayer for the kingdom its full realism and urgency. It follows, however, that what such a petition did for them, in their unique position of being in at the beginning of something of which they were to see the end, it can never do again for others at a later date who can never be in that position, even though the petition is written down for them in the Lord's Prayer. Whatever the words "till he come" may now mean and do for the modern Christian—and it is by no means clear what that is—it cannot be precisely what they meant and did for the Christians to whom Paul wrote them, for part of the urgency in their case was generated by the confidence that the final instalments of what they were to receive through Christ would not tarry long behind the first instalments which they had already received. If they had contemplated in advance the centuries which we now know to have supervened, their faith could not have had the particular quality it did have. It would seem that this end of the world note acted, so to say, as the booster rocket to get the Gospel into orbit, and that once in orbit the rocket apparatus had to be jettisoned. Here and there in the New Testament we see evidence of this jettisoning.[10] Nevertheless, the Gospel remains fundamentally the same, and this is an indication that the primary purpose of this kind of language is not to pronounce upon the mysteries of time, but to move men to take God with complete seriousness as beginning, middle, and end, and to direct their gaze towards him so that they care to the uttermost about his will.

This leads us far and wide over the teaching of Jesus, for the accent of finality lies on so much that he says, making God really God and God's claim absolute. In the Jewish religion there were two strands which were in danger of becoming separated, each going off on its own. First there was this end of the world thinking, which was concerned with the mystery of God and his world, and about the means by which he would bring the world to the goal he had in mind in creating it. Such thinking became increasingly fantastic and removed from reality. The blessed consummation was placed in the heavens, and language was violently strained to depict it. Secondly there was the ethic of the Jewish religion. This had had its origin in the teaching of the prophets, where God's commands had their ground and basis not in themselves but in the mystery of the God whose commands they were, but there was a tendency to make these commands a moral system standing on its own feet and to be observed for its own sake.

Jesus brings these two strands together again in a remarkable unity, the one to be at the service of the other. End of the world thinking is not to arouse fantastic speculations, but to bring men face to face with the ultimate demands of God stated in their most radical form, and in his will is their creation, destiny, and moral life. Thus there are parables and statements of the kingdom not as something which comes or is entered, but as that which confronts a man with the demand for the sacrifice of all that he has for it, and to which he had better not commit himself if he cannot see it through,* which is a crisis putting his whole life at stake,† which completely reverses the normal standards and judgements by which men govern their lives,‡ which can only be a curse to those who rest in the pride of human possession, but a blessing to those who out of their lack look to God as their sole sufficiency.§ In the gospel as a whole these are not general truths about God's kingdom wherever it may manifest itself, but embodied truths which walk abroad in Jesus' own ruthless demands upon men for discipleship, his fierce judgement upon the Pharisees for their pride of possession, and his relentless and compassionate pursuit of the outcast.‖

* Matt. 13.45f; Luke 14.28ff. † Luke 16.1–8; 12.16–20.
‡ Matt. 20.1–16. § Luke 16.19–31; 15.11–32.
‖ Luke 9.57–62; Matt. 21.28–32; Mark 2.15ff.

39

The same accent is heard in his treatment of the moral law. He takes the law of Moses as the hallowed instrument of the rule of God in Israel, and affirms it: to love God with the whole self, and the neighbour as the self, is the whole duty of man. What that means, however, is now stated in such a way that the full demand of God in it is made clear and inescapable. It is thrust into the marrow of human life so that it can go no further. When the prohibition of murder is interpreted as prohibition of anger, and adultery is defined as lust in the heart, and the love of the neighbour is pushed until it becomes love of the enemy, then the moral law has reached its goal, and there is no possible situation which is not related to the rule of God.*

There are no new precepts in the teaching of Jesus but only the old, and the old are so stated that it is impossible to make out of his teaching an ethical system. Rather it is the end of all ethical systems as we generally understand them, and will blow them all up. The same accent is heard again in his treatment of religion which means in the context of Judaism the threefold obligation of fasting, prayer, and almsgiving. These duties are taken over and not elaborated. He does not teach a new technique of prayer, or give rules for fasting, or a programme of almsgiving. He says one thing about each, and it is the same thing. Each is to be performed in such a way that what it has as its goal, a total adherence to God, is made plain thereby. Prayer is to be prayer in secret, so as to escape any evaluation except from the Father who alone sees in secret; fasting is to be done in such a way that men are deceived, and only God can see what it is good for; alms-

* Matt. 5.21–48.

40

giving is to be so uncalculated that even the giver is deceived and only God knows its worth. Acts of piety of any other kind are acts done before men, and have men as their goal, and so contradict their nature and purpose, which is to secure a total adherence to God.[11]

The petition "Thy will be done" in Matthew's version, even if not original, and even if in danger of introducing an element of repetition in so brief and concentrated a prayer, has nevertheless a certain fitness as both reinforcing the petition for the kingdom, and as adding something inward to it.[12] It reinforces the petition for the kingdom because the will of God has also this end of the world note. It is the final will of God that none of his little ones should perish* and that the disciples shall be given the kingdom.† The context of the prayer of Jesus himself in Gethsemane shows the temptation which he undergoes there to be not simply *a* temptation, but *the* temptation which has the destiny of the world at stake, and the prayer uttered there "not what I will but what thou wilt" is not simply *a* prayer for the performance of one amongst other moral duties, but a prayer for the doing of *the* final will which preserves the world. The addition to this petition of the words "as in heaven so on earth" points in the same direction. These words can mean "as God's will is perfectly done in heaven, so may it be done on earth", and this is the only possible meaning of the English version "on earth, as it is in heaven"; but a more probable translation both of the Greek and the Latin is "both in heaven and on earth", heaven and earth being a biblical expression for the whole creation.[13] The petition is then that God will bring about for his whole creation, in a

* Matt. 18.14.   † Luke 12.32.

final and total form, the end which he had in mind in its beginning. The petition "Do thou cause thy will to be done throughout the whole creation" adds, however, a certain interior and ethical note which pertains more to the word "will" than to the word "kingdom".[14] The finality of the rule of God, which brings history to an end, is not an arbitrary decree about the world and its destiny; it is linked with the finality of the will of God, which is final because it is the expression of the righteousness, truth, and love which God is in himself.

Christian prayer, as it is informed by the Lord's Prayer, like Christian life, as it is informed by Jesus' teaching, is total and final—total as involving the whole self, and final as concerned with the ultimate and perfect will of God. That teaching is relevant to human life only as first appearing to us as irrelevant. Its immediate concern is not with to-day or to-morrow, or with any calculable series of days, but with the end of the days, and with to-day and to-morrow in relation to that end. It serves the concerns of everyday only by first ignoring them and passing them by, and in occupying itself with the final things, with perfection. It does not come down to our needs as we ordinarily conceive them, but insists that first we come up to where it is. It takes up a position from which all else is relegated to the secondary position where it rightly belongs, and from which it may be seen in its proper proportions. Dr Johnson's dictum that "when a man knows that he is to be hanged in a fortnight, it concentrates his mind wonderfully" is a secular version of this Christian truth. The unity of the teaching of Jesus is not that of a system of ethics with some superior evaluation of what is good and what is bad; it lies in the consistency with which, each time he opens his mouth, it is to bring men to a position where they take God and the radical demands of his kingdom and his will with complete seriousness. This is the position out of which they are to pray.

4

The Bread

LITURGIES, and prayers within liturgies, generally exhibit a pattern and design, and a whole theology or spiritual outlook can be conveyed through them. It is the function of liturgiologists to study such patterns, and perhaps to write new liturgies or prayers according to what seems to them a proper pattern. Has the Lord's Prayer a pattern or design? Is there anything inevitable about the petitions of which it is made up, and do they together constitute a whole, or is each petition to be taken by itself without reference to the rest?[1] The versions of both Matthew and Luke are said, when turned back into Aramaic, to have a rhythmic structure, but this of itself does not establish a design, and differences of structure, as the presence or absence of the petitions "thy will be done" and "deliver us from the evil", as also later the addition of the doxology, could carry with them differences of design. Some have been so impressed by parallels between the Lord's Prayer and Jewish models as to conclude that the former is for the most part a cento, mosaic, or patchwork of phrases from these models, or has been amplified from a shorter form by additions from them or from the gospel tradition. Against this is the judgement of the Jewish scholar C. G. Montefiore that while the prayer is not original in ideas it is "original in

44

the choice of ideas, and in their grouping. Whoever put it together chose with fine religious feeling and insight". [2] This question is one which would naturally be raised either at the outset or when the whole prayer has been reviewed, but it is raised in fact by the petition for bread.

In the *Eighteen Benedictions* there is a prayer for a fruitful year which stands at the end of the first group of petitions, those, namely, which are concerned with man's temporal needs, and immediately before those concerned with the future salvation of Israel. [3] In the Lord's Prayer it is the other way round. The first group is concerned with the future saving work of God, and the prayer for bread stands at a point of transition from the two (in Matthew three) petitions for God to bring about what pertains to himself alone as God (thy name, thy kingdom, thy will) to the three (in Matthew four) petitions which pray for certain consequent effects for men (our bread, our debts, lead us not, deliver us). These latter are, unlike the former, bound together into a single whole by being connected with "and". Thus the petition for bread would seem to mark a division of the Prayer into two parts. What is the relation between the parts? What kind of a petition is this that it should stand first in the second part, and what is the design of the Prayer as a whole that a petition for bread should be thought the most fitting to follow on immediately from the all-embracing petitions concerning God's name, kingdom, and will?

This petition appears to be, and is commonly regarded as, the simplest of all. Here at any rate we might suppose that we are safe from the prying hands of the critic, and from the complications which he so often introduces. But it is not so. On the contrary, it turns out on examination to be the most difficult of all, and the most uncertain in its meaning. It is one of the most debated sentences in the gospels, and the literature of the debate is immense and continues to grow. The petition is unique in the Prayer as being the only one to contain an adjective. That in itself is noteworthy in a prayer which is so brief and succinct, and in which not a word is wasted. Adjectives can be tricky things, and the Bible is comparatively restrained in its use of them, confining itself on the whole to a few of well-established meaning. The simplest and most precise mode of statement is the combination of noun and verb. Adjectives, as descriptive modifications of the noun, can introduce an element of imprecision into the sentence, which is the more serious if the meaning of the sentence hangs on the precise modification of the noun which the adjective makes.

Such is the case in this petition, where in the Greek the adjective stands at the beginning, and not as in the English versions at the end, of the sentence. The prayer is for bread, but what kind of a prayer it is depends on the answer to the question, "What kind of bread?" The answer to that depends on the meaning of the adjective, and—here is the surprise—no one knows for certain what the adjective means. The word translated "daily" is a Greek word which transliterated is *epiousios*, and the problem, as Origen already knew, is what this word means. When he reached this petition in his commentary on the Lord's Prayer he wrote as follows: "Give us this day our ἐπιούσιος bread, or as Luke has it, Give us day by day our ἐπιούσιος bread. Since some suppose that we are bidden to pray for corporeal bread, it is fitting to remove the false opinion they create through this interpretation, and to establish the truth concerning 'ἐπιούσιος bread'. . . . We must now also grasp the meaning of ἐπιούσιος. And the first thing to be realized is this, that the word ἐπιούσιος is not used by any of the Greeks, or philosophers, nor is it in general use in the customary vocabulary of ordinary people, but it seems to have been invented by the Evangelists. At least both Matthew and Luke agree about it without any difference at all and use it. . . . Very similar to the word ἐπιούσιος is a word written by Moses as spoken by God, Ye shall be unto me a περιούσιος (A.V. peculiar) people (Ex. 19.5). And both words seem to me to have been derived from οὐσία (substance), the one indicating bread which is united in the Substance, and the other signifying the people which lives close to (περί) the Substance and shares therein."[4]

We are not concerned with Origen's interpretation of the word, which depends on his philosophical mind, and is certainly fanciful. What concerns us is the remarkable fact that Origen, who was one of the most learned men of his time, and an outstanding linguist, was able to affirm that the word *epiousios* nowhere occurred in Greek literature, and that, so far as he was aware, it was not in common use in the Greek of everyday speech. In suggesting that the evangelists coined the word he seems to say that he was unaware of its existence anywhere else. Being helped to understand the word neither by written nor by spoken Greek he had to fall back on what he could deduce from what he believed to be the derivation of the word.

Are we any better off than Origen? Not as regards Greek literature, as only a portion of what Origen knew has come down to us, and such as has come down to us that was written after Origen's time does not offer any

47

instance of the word. What of the vocabulary of ordinary people? Our knowledge of this vocabulary has been greatly extended in recent years by the discovery in the sands of Egypt, which are alone dry enough to preserve them intact for two thousand years, of great quantities of papyri, mostly in fragments. These are of many different kinds—letters, accounts, petitions, receipts, wills, and all sorts of other contents of Egyptian waste-paper baskets. In 1889 Flinders Petrie published in a book called *Hawara, Biamu and Arsinoe* the text of a papyrus account book from Upper Egypt. The papyrus has since been lost and cannot now be rechecked, but one item in the list of accounts read: "$\frac{1}{2}$ obol for epiousi . . .". The word is either broken off or an abbreviation, like other abbreviations in the list. It will then probably be an abbreviation for *epiousion* and the meaning will be, "Half an obol's worth of epiousian things". Here is an instance of the word in common speech, though there is nothing to indicate what it means. But in an inscription on a wall in Pompeii there has also been discovered an expenditure list which contains as one of its items, "Five asses for diaria". Now *diaria* is Latin for daily rations, and it is suggested that the two are equivalent expressions. If so, it would establish the meaning "daily" for *epiousios*. Unfortunately the evidence remains tantalizingly uncertain, and can hardly be said to have settled the question. It is not proven that ἐπιούσιος and *diaria* are the Greek and Latin for the same thing. Some have objected that half an obol is too small a sum for a daily ration, and have suggested that the word denotes something small, "bare necessities" perhaps.[5] The papyrus is from the fifth century A.D., two centuries after Origen and four centuries after the word began to be used in the Prayer in the Church, and it cannot be ruled out that its constant repetition in the Church in the sense "daily", which it undoubtedly came to have there, had led to this meaning being attached to its ordinary use. That is, the Lord's Prayer would illuminate the papyrus and not vice versa.[6] It may be that another papyrus will turn up which will put the matter beyond doubt, but also maybe not. In the meantime we are still much in the position of Origen, and are driven back to an attempt to get at its meaning by guessing at its derivation.

This was done in some detail by Bishop Lightfoot at the time of the making of the Revised Version, and, as with all his work, it has hardly been improved upon since.[7] There are two possibilities, each of which can give a number of meanings. The first is that the word is derived from ἐπί and ἰέναι, the verb "to come" or "to go", giving such meanings as "what comes upon", "future", "regularly recurring", "following on", and since the participle from this verb was used with the word "day" to mean "the coming day" *epiousios* could perhaps mean "for the coming day", or "sufficient for the coming day". Then the prayer would be for the bread of the coming day, i.e. for the next day, if prayed at night, and for the dawning day if prayed in the early morning.[8] The second possibility is that preferred by Origen (though he drew his own peculiar conclusions from it), namely that it is derived from ἐπί and εἶναι, the verb "to be", yielding such meanings as "what belongs to our sustenance", "what pertains to existence", "for the present", "sufficient", "necessary".[9] Lightfoot was clear that considerations of word formation made the first derivation preferable, and that considerations of sense made it more likely.[10]

Is there any help to be gained from the earliest translations of the Greek New Testament into other languages? How do the translators, who stood nearer to spoken Greek than we can, show by their translations that they understood the word? Here again there is much uncertainty. In the Eastern part of the Church the oldest Syriac versions have a word which in Syriac means "continual", and the Revised Version of the Syriac has a word meaning "of our necessity". Of the Egyptian versions one (the Sahidic) has "coming", another (the Memphitic) has "of the morrow".[11]

In the Western part of the Church the situation was curious. The greatest Christian scholar after Origen was St Jerome (A.D. 345–420), and one of the scholarly tasks which he undertook, at the request of his bishop, Pope Damasus, was to make a revision of the various Latin translations of the Scriptures which were current by his time in the West. The result of his work, which he did with reference to Greek and Hebrew originals, was the Vulgate, from that time the official version of the Bible in the West, as it is still of the Roman Church to-day. In the Old Latin versions Jerome found the word ἐπιούσιον rendered by *cotidianum*, the Latin word for "daily", and in Luke's version of the Prayer he left it so. But clearly he was not happy about it, and in Matthew's version he substituted the word *supersubstantialem*, and it so comes about that the Roman Church has two versions of this petition in the Prayer. Jerome's choice of this word shows that he thought that ἐπιούσιος was derived from ἐπί and οὐσία (substance), and he explains that he meant

by the word "above all substances", "super-excellent".
But further, when commenting on this petition in his
commentary on Matthew's Gospel, he says that in the
Gospel according to the Hebrews (a lost gospel in
Aramaic, possibly a translation of our Gospel according
to Matthew into that language, and also called the Gospel
of the Nazarenes because it was, says Jerome, in use among
the Nazarenes, by whom he means the Aramaic speaking
Jewish Christians of Palestine and Syria), he had found
the bread described by the word *mahar*, which, he says,
means "for to-morrow, and that means future".[12]
Hence, he says, the bread for to-morrow was not earthly
bread but the bread of life.

Thus the early translations do not settle the matter
either, but only serve to show that by the time they were
made there was already confusion and uncertainty as to
what the Greek word meant. One can only suppose that
it was a word somehow peculiar to the vocabulary of the
Church in the earliest days, that it was used to express
something special for which none of the ordinary words
about bread would suffice, that its special meaning was
lost, that it was thought in some areas to mean "daily",
and that this meaning prevailed. When we use it in this
sense we are again leaning heavily upon the tradition of
the Church.

It is a remarkable fact that there should be an uncertainty of this kind at the very heart of the Lord's
Prayer and in what appears to be its simplest petition.
This may serve as a warning to Christians against over-
dogmatism, and as a reminder that in the faith as they have
received it a confident belief in God is not incompatible
with a considerable measure of agnosticism about this

or that element in it. In this situation one can only state what seems to one to be more probable and to give reasons. The rendering "daily" has some formidable objections to it. The first has to do with our judgement of the design and tenor of the Prayer as a whole. The petitions which precede that for bread are concerned with God's final works—his hallowing his name, his causing his kingdom to come, and his will to be done. It will be suggested later that this is also the character of the petitions which follow. They are also prayers for the final gifts of God as they affect men, and which belong to the last days—the forgiveness of sins before the judgement, immunity from the final trial of strength between God and evil, and deliverance from the evil one. If the whole of the rest of the Prayer were of this kind, a petition which suddenly in the middle descended to the needs of everyday would be isolated. It would certainly suggest that the Prayer has no design, but is a collection of individual petitions, each to be taken on its own.[13] This petition is also a prayer for what God is to give. Is it a prayer simply for God's general providence in sustaining the world to continue, or is it a prayer suited to the special conditions of the disciples of Jesus, and for a kind of bread which is specially the gift of God?

The second objection is that if *epiousios* means "daily" it is difficult to escape the conclusion that the petition is tautologous, i.e. it says the same thing twice by using two similar words of time in a single sentence—"Our daily bread give us to-day" (Matthew), or "Our daily bread give us daily" (Luke). This is a serious matter, especially in a prayer where otherwise not a single word is otiose. Thirdly, it may be held that the very rarity of the word, which has given rise to such uncertainty over its meaning, argues that it was expressing something special and closely related to peculiar features of the Gospel.

Suppose we were to consider the rendering "of the coming day", "of the morrow", which in Lightfoot's view was the more likely as regards derivation, which has some support in the versions, and which is the interpretation of the Gospel according to the Hebrews mentioned by Jerome. It would seem that this rendering might light up Matthew's version, though not so much Luke's. In Matthew's version the order of the words in the petition is striking. Literally it runs, "Our bread, our epiousian bread, give us to-day." An adverb of time is not normally the last word in a sentence unless it is intended to be emphatic. "Give us *to-day*". If it is so here, then does "to-day" stand in contrast to something else which is not "to-day"—"to-morrow", perhaps? Then there would be two notes of time in a single sentence which would not constitute it a tautology, because the second would not be repeating the first but would be in sharp contrast with it, and the point would be in the contrast—"Our bread of to-morrow give us to-day".[14] But would there have been any point in the disciples praying such a prayer? What would it have been supposed to mean?

It must be remembered that the faith of the New Testament was produced on the basis of the Old Testament. The salvation in Christ was the fulfilment of God's promises to his people and of his ways with men, and the Old Testament contained not only the promises, but models of how God goes about the work of salvation. There would be a new exodus, not now from the slavery of Egypt or the captivity of Babylon, but from evil; God would make a new covenant with his people and write a new law in their hearts, and there would be a true sabbath rest in a new Promised Land. In this pattern of redemption there had been a significant incident concerning bread, when God had himself given men bread, and had given it in such a way that they had to-morrow's bread to-day. This was the incident of the manna.* This was a special bread, called in the Old Testament the bread of heaven, or the bread which God gives.[15] It was a sign of God's ability to sustain them after he had redeemed them. It was also a sign of the faith and trust of the Israelites in God's ability that on the eve of the sabbath they were to gather "on the sixth day the bread of two days", the bread for to-morrow to-day.[16] We do not know how far the manna and the sabbath, and manna for the sabbath, were images for Jesus and his disciples of the joy of the coming age, when God will hallow his name and cause his kingdom to come.[17] We do have mention in the gospels of eating bread in the kingdom of God, and of a mysterious loaf which will suffice the disciples, and which is a foretaste of the heavenly banquet.† The miracles of the feeding of the five thousand and of the four thousand may perhaps best be understood as anticipations of Jesus' feeding his disciples with the bread of heaven, and this is clearly the way in which the fourth evangelist interpreted them.[18]

If the petition in the Lord's Prayer were for the bread of to-morrow to-day, that is, for the heavenly sabbath

* Ex. 16; Num. 11.4-9; Neh. 9.15-20.
† Luke 14.15; Mark 8.14-21; 14.22 and parallels; Matt. 8.11= Luke 13.29.

bread of the kingdom which had already drawn near, then it would fit the design of the Prayer as a whole if that prayer is for the final things of God, and would explain why prayer concerning the name, the kingdom, and the will should be immediately followed by prayer for bread. The same level would be maintained throughout. To pray that God will hallow his name and bring his kingdom is the prayer of men whose appetites are whetted thereby, so that nothing short of divine nourishment will suffice.

If this interpretation is allowed, then the petition is not for bare necessities, or an act of trust in God's ability to supply whatever shall be needful. It rather places at the heart of Christian faith desire, and the prospect of enjoyment and fruition. It is undoubtedly *agapē*, love in the sense of the self-giving of God to men in Christ and the self-giving of men to one another through Christ, which is pre-eminent in the New Testament, but it is possible so to concentrate upon it as to obscure the place of a love which is rooted in desire, and of the promise of satisfaction and repletion conveyed in terms of eating and drinking, music and light, a city and a country, stature and vitality, and the resplendence of glory.[19] There are deep denials in the New Testament which cut to the bone, but they are not ends in themselves, but means to an end, which is a fullness of life beggaring description. It is impossible to eliminate the motive of reward from the teaching of Jesus, though, of course, the reward, to be a true reward, is to be commensurate with the activity of which it is the reward; indeed, it is that activity in its consummated form.[20] In this also the New Testament is cradled in the Old. There God's covenant with his people, his love and discipline of them, are accompanied by the prospect of a consummation which is unashamedly represented in material terms. Devotion to the covenant and the commandments will lead to a land flowing with milk and honey and with all good things.* If later the rewards are spoken of in what we would call more spiritual terms, this is not by escape or divorce from the material, but by expanding it until it speaks of a desire which takes the fullness of divine life to satisfy.[21] Material things furnish a rich vocabulary through which to grasp the possible union of the life of the creature with the Creator. Geography symbolizes in Canaan a country in which man is fully at home, politics in Sion a city which has the foundations and whose maker and builder is God;† and if the lesson has to be learnt that man does not live by bread alone but by every word from the mouth of God, it is learnt through an actual physical hunger being appeased by manna, the bread supplied by God himself. This wealth of images is displayed refashioned in Christ particularly in the Revelation of John, and included in them is the promise to him that overcomes of the gift of the hidden manna, and of Christ's coming in to dine with him who opens the door.‡

* Deut. 6.3 and *passim*.   † Heb. 4.1–10; 11.8ff, 14ff; Rev. 21.
‡ Rev. 2.17; 3.20.

5

Forgive, Preserve, Deliver

If the Lord's Prayer is more than a collection of individual petitions lying side by side, and if we are not reading into it when we take it as exhibiting a unity of design, then its brevity is presumably due to its concentration on the essential verities. The man of God is not to go around with piles of unnecessary luggage. But "design" may be too literary a word to apply; rather the Prayer is a single jet with its end already in its beginning. For after the petition for the disciples' fruition of the bread of the kingdom, which itself arises from the petitions for God's final works, his hallowing of his name, his causing his kingdom to come and his will to be done, only one thing further is said, and the two (in Matthew three) petitions which follow are in fact variations on this one thing. The prayers for remission of debts, for immunity from temptation, and for deliverance from the evil one are all concerned, in this way or that, and in an ascending order of complexity, with what stands in the way of that fruition and of entry into the kingdom when it comes. They reveal the reason for the previous petitions, and for the form they take, to lie not simply in the necessary requests which sons should make for their father's providential care—a kind of spiritual good manners— but in the existence of a dark underside of the world, of an irrational surd in the universe, which the New Testament in one passage with admirable but terrifying reserve calls "the mystery of iniquity".*

The difficulty here is the extreme opaqueness of the subject matter. Such shafts of light as may penetrate it from the Gospel of Christ do not add up to a Christian solution of the problem of evil, for there is no such thing, though we may hope that some rays of illumination may come from a Christian grappling with evil itself. The problem is how to understand the language with which we grope about in this dark matter, so as to be able to pray these petitions with conviction and with spiritual integrity.

The first of the three petitions is for forgiveness of sins, in the form of the cancellation of debts. This is completely so in Matthew's version, "Remit us our debts, as we also have remitted to our debtors", which is evidently more original than Luke's version, "Forgive us our sins, as we also remit to us every one who is indebted to us", since the latter, while it has "forgive us our sins" in the first part, reverts to the metaphor of debt in the second part, but in a more generalized and secondary form "as we also remit to every one who is indebted to us".[1] "Remit" was used sufficiently often in the Old Testament with "sins" in the sense of "forgive" to make it easy to substitute the religious, more conventional "forgive us our sins" for the more vivid "cancel us our debts".

Although the idea of sin as indebtedness was not rare, this sentence in Matthew is the only place in the Bible where the actual word "debt" is used for sin. It appears

* 2 Thess. 2.7 (A.V.).

to be a contribution to our religious vocabulary from Aramaic, in which one word does for both. It lives for a brief time in the vocabulary of Jesus,* but drops out of the language of the Christian Church and is continued only in that of the rabbis.[2] It is a financial metaphor. Man falls into arrears and piles up an overdraft; God writes it off and cancels it.[3]

This analogy of debt and its cancellation is not the only way of talking about evil and what God does in face of it, nor is it the most profound. In the New Testament there are other conceptions, such as reconciliation, sacrifice, recreation, justification, which go more to the heart of the matter, and reveal more deeply the relation between God and man.[4] Indeed, the forgiveness of sins, which is the more conventionally religious form of the cancellation of debts, is not as frequent in the New Testament as might be supposed from the place it came to occupy, and still occupies, in Christian thought and language, where it tends to take over.[5] In all his epistles Paul has the phrase only once;† in the Johannine writings there are three references to it, in the Gospel the post-resurrection gift to the apostles of the remission of sins, and in the First Epistle the statements that God forgives for Jesus' sake and in pursuance of his faithfulness and justice.‡ The Synoptic Gospels have in common the healing of the paralytic with its "Son, thy sins be forgiven thee", and similar to it is Luke's story of the sinful woman.§ Matthew alone has the forgiveness of sins attached to the blood of Jesus at the Last Supper, and Mark and

* Matt. 18.24–34; Luke 7.41; 13.4.   † Col. 1.14 (also Eph. 1.7)
‡ John 20.23; 1 John 1.9; 2.12.
§ Mark 2.5–12 and parallels; Luke 7.48.

Luke to the baptism of John.* Only in Luke's writings does the phrase become at all frequent, where it is something of a formal summary, first of the object of the earthly life of Jesus, and then of the gift of God to men through the exalted Christ and his work.† Thus "the forgiveness of sins" has a limited place in the vocabulary of the New Testament, and it is a limited expression for the subject it is talking about. Nevertheless, it is chosen for this representative position in the Lord's Prayer.

In what does the debt consist, and in what is its remission? In one sense all men are always and entirely in God's debt, because they owe all that they have and are to God. There is nothing we possess we have not first received.‡ Man's life is loaned to him by God or borrowed by him from God; "This night is thy soul [life] required [back] from thee."§ Clearly this is not what is intended here, since men ought not to pray, and cannot pray, to be remitted this debt.[6] It is one way of describing the permanent relation of creature to Creator, and this relation cannot be dissolved. To seek to dissolve it would be itself sin. What lies here behind the thought of debt is not our existence as such, but the fact that we exist for something. Life is not simply loaned to us; it is life of a certain kind which is given—and it is given for something. It is the failure to fulfil this something which constitutes the debt.

Human life is only human as it is life in relationship with, and responsibility towards, God. The humanity of human life is known in Israel, where the covenant re-

---

* Matt. 26.28; Mark 1.4=Luke 3.3.

† Luke 1.77; 4.18; 24.47; Acts 2.38; 5.31; 10.43; 13.38; 26.18.

‡ 1 Cor. 4.7.   § Luke 12.20.

lationship with God determines men's existence, and makes of it existence for something. In the covenant is a mutual obligation of love and loyalty. On God's side is the obligation to be God to this people, and on the people's side is the obligation to the will of God, in which their truly human life consists, and to God's law as their instruction in this life.* Men fail to meet this obligation; they fall into arrears of duty. This is the debt. Further, in distinction from some forms of Jewish piety, which envisaged the possibility that the debt might be offset by a sufficient number of other obligations met, what is meant here is a permanent indebtedness and an inability to pay. This creates an impasse with only one way out, which is from God's side by his cancellation of the debt. He writes it off, as he is also said in the Scriptures not to remember men's sins any more.† Such a cancellation conveys his love for men to them in the form of grace, that is, as a free gift; it is the form his faithfulness and loyalty, his justice and love, take in face of the failure of men in their obligation, and it renews his covenant with them. On man's side, through this cancellation his very failure can become the means of a renewal of his love and loyalty to God, who is known even more as the God he is through his generous act.

Limited as debt and its cancellation may be in comparison with other analogies for sin and for God's dealing with it, in one respect they are more effective, and this may account for their choice in the Prayer. The very idea of debt, especially in the plural, as here, "remit us our debts", presupposes an account. Only when the account is made up can the debts be established. Debt does not

* Cf. Deut. 26.17ff.　　　† Ps. 25.7; Isa. 43.25; 64.9; Jer. 31.34.

speak primarily of how men stand at any one moment, as do guilt, uncleanness, transgression, disobedience, or breach of fellowship, but of how they stand when the sum is done and the reckoning made. It relates sin and forgiveness to the end of things, with which the Prayer seems to be concerned throughout. The prayer for remission is the prayer of those who have been made by the thought of God's name, kingdom, and will to stand at the end of things, and from there to ask from God what they know they cannot supply to themselves, the removal of the obstacles to their enjoyment of his final and perfect gifts. This has a bearing on the second half of the petition, "as we remit to our debtors".

This is the only petition in the Prayer which has a qualifying clause attached, or which contemplates any necessary co-operation with God on the part of men. There are two difficulties in this qualification. The first is that the same word "debt" is used both of the relationship of ourselves to God and of others to ourselves. In the first case, however, it expresses our relationship by reason of our total obligation to him as God and of our failure in it. Can it be said of others that they have this same relation to us? Are we in a position to play God to them? This can only begin to be true between those who know themselves to be members of a community which is in this world but is of another world, and which lives in time by reference to the end of time. The law of this community is that obligations of love are due between the sons of God of a total kind, the failure to honour which is debt, and the readiness to cancel the debt is to reproduce as sons the character of the Father.* Only by so doing

* Matt. 5.43–8.

62

can men be in the condition where the enjoyment of divine things is possible.

The second difficulty is one of spiritual integrity. "There is", writes Charles Williams, "a tendency among some Christians to make a burden of things which non-Christians would pass over lightly. They overdo forgiveness, as they overdo patience and the other virtues."[7] It is, he continues, a matter of spiritual courtesy and good manners not to assume too easily or too quickly that there is anything that needs to be forgiven. It simply is not true that I, or anyone else, except a psychopath, wakes every morning with a burning sense of multiple injury and of the need of my forgiving it, however much the daily recital of the Lord's Prayer might be held to encourage me to think so. I am hardly aware of a single debt owing to me over the past how many years. I may be aware that I owe debts of this kind to others which need remission by them, but on that score the Prayer says nothing. How then am I to repeat this petition with conviction? Here again Matthew's version seems preferable to Luke's, in which the petition, like his petition for the bread, has been generalized for daily use. In Matthew the petition runs "Remit us our debts, as we also have remitted to our debtors." The verbs are again in the aorist, and they make the petition read like the statement of those who announce that they have made a once and for all renunciation of all debts owed to them, and who therefore present themselves as in a condition to receive the same treatment from God.

"And lead us not into temptation." There are two difficulties also attaching to this petition which have to be faced if it is to be repeated whole-heartedly. The first was apparent already to Tertullian. "That our supplication", he wrote, "might be not only for the forgiveness but also for the total removal of wrong-doings, he added LEAD US NOT INTO TEMPTATION." And then Tertullian himself adds—"that is, suffer us not to be led, of course by the one who does tempt. For God forbid that the Lord should be supposed to tempt, as though he were either ignorant of each man's faith or desirous of overthrowing it".[8] Tertullian may not have been the first to gloss the petition in this way, and he was certainly not the last. St Cyprian in his commentary on the Lord's Prayer repeats Tertullian's gloss, "suffer us not to be led", only not now as an explanation, but as part of the text of the Prayer itself,[9] and two centuries later St Augustine in his commentary on the Prayer could write that many in his day prayed the petition in this form, and that he had found it so in some Latin manuscripts.[10] But while some passages in Scripture could be appealed to in support of this gloss,* nevertheless in some of the great temptations of the Old Testament God is himself said to be the tempter, and this is the plain meaning of the words here.

The second difficulty is that at the natural, and even at a highly moral and spiritual level, temptation is not something to be avoided, but rather something to be sought, or at any rate welcomed. "Let the lad win his spurs", and if he is to do so he must try out his strength against the opposition. If I brought up my child in a germ free atmosphere, he would catch a fatal disease the first time he travelled in a railway carriage. Temptation as a test of character, as a means of purifying the soul, as a means of spiritual progress, this is how temptation is treated in one

* Jas. 1.13ff; 1 Cor. 10.13.

excellent manual of Christian spirituality.[11] On this level the prayer should rather be "lead us into temptation", and this is what one of the psalmists does say, "Examine me, O Lord, and prove me; try my reins and my heart."* Both James and Peter can exhort their readers to rejoice when they fall into manifold temptations, since temptation tests character and produces the quality of endurance, and Paul says much the same.† These two difficulties can only be solved together by considering what the temptation is of which God is said to be the author, and why it is to be avoided.

The Greek word translated "tempt" means to put to the test,[12] and this putting to the test may be of two kinds, reflecting two levels of evil. There is temptation as we generally think of it and are aware of it in terms of the moral struggle, a suggestion from within or without which inclines or pulls us to choose the worse rather than the better, our own pleasure rather than the good of another or the good pleasure of God. This is on the same plane as sin regarded as debt and as the failure to render to God and others their due. But there is in the Scriptures temptation of a more radical kind when the stakes are higher. This is the trial when men are pressed to deny God altogether, to defect completely from him, and to attempt to ground life on some other basis than its relation to him. It is part of the mystery of iniquity that this is a possibility open to the creature, and it is part of the opaqueness of this mystery that it is the height of irrationality that men who hang upon God for their very existence should reject the God who is their sole *raison d'être*.

* Ps. 26.2.   † Jas. 1.2ff; 1 Pet. 1.6–9; Rom. 5.3ff.

The great temptations are represented as temptations from God of this kind. The temptation of Adam is to eat of the tree of the knowledge of good and evil and so to know and become as God. This is not one temptation amongst others, but the temptation which attacks the very basis of human existence, and seeks to introduce a contradiction at its heart. To know evil without doing it is the prerogative of God alone; for men to grasp at it is to try to play God to themselves, and to fall altogether from the creaturely state. Knowing evil they inevitably choose it as their good.[13] The temptation of Abraham is not simply one temptation amongst others, but the temptation of the archetypal man of faith. The fulfilment of God's own promise that he shall through his seed inherit the world depends for its fulfilment on the continued existence of his only son Isaac, and now God tempts him by commanding him to give up Isaac in sacrifice. The temptations of Israel by God in the wilderness are temptations of the people which is called God's son to defect altogether by doubting God's capacity to keep going the state of freedom and happiness into which he has brought them by redemption. The temptation of Job, carried out by Satan with the permission of God, is his reduction to the last extremity to make him curse God. After this there are only the temptations of Jesus. These also are not temptations as we ordinarily think of and experience them. They are recapitulations of the temptations of Israel, to revolt against God through hunger, to put God himself to the test, for which Moses was forbidden the Promised Land, and to compromise with the world, so losing the holiness which God had given;[14] only now their force is redoubled as the temptations of one who really and truly is God's Son, and upon his conquest of them depends the possibility of men adhering to God.

Temptation thus takes on a different colour from the private enticement of the individual to disobedience of one of the commandments. In the book of Daniel, and in the thought of others like him, temptation becomes the word for a trial which is of cosmic proportions, a "tribulation", as it is called, of a final kind, when the whole force of Satan's power is to be hurled against God's saints to seduce them and break their allegiance.* It can only be described in terms of upheaval, chaos, and terror in the universe. By it God brings to an issue the conflict between his own order and the disorder of evil. This kind of thinking is reproduced in the teaching of Jesus as it has been assembled in his instructions to the disciples immediately before his passion, when he speaks of a tribulation so great that no human being could survive if God did not shorten the days, and he accompanies the instruction with the urgent command to watch.† When therefore Jesus in Gethsemane repeats the petition of the Lord's Prayer in the form of a command, "Watch and pray that ye enter not into temptation", and when he himself is in an extreme agony of prayer, we are probably to understand that this particular temptation, this time of extreme tribulation, has begun. The hour of which he had said that no one knew it has now come, and has come because the Son of Man is to be delivered into the hands of sinners.[15] For the Son of Man who is the very embodiment of God's saints, and the Son of God who is God's obedient one, to be rejected by the world is the extreme

* Dan. 12.1ff.   † Mark 13.14–23.

67

upheaval of God's order and the supreme irrationality. Jesus himself goes into this temptation, first in imagination through prayer and then in actuality in his passion, but he alone is able to do so, and he does so on behalf of his disciples. God no doubt in some way past their understanding has the situation in hand, but for them there is no room for moral attitudes or heroics. The disciple is simply to pray that God, in bringing matters to an issue, will preserve him immune from this temptation.

Luke's version of the Prayer ends on this negative note; Matthew's does not. A further petition is added, which is not, however, a separate and independent petition, but the positive counterpart of the previous negative, closely coupled to it by "but". The nature of the temptation is further shown by the fact that to be kept immune from it is to be snatched from the hands of Satan. The noun rendered "evil" can in Greek be either neuter or masculine. The English versions, following a tradition of interpretation at least as old as St Augustine, take it as neuter and render it by the abstract "evil", but the matter has often been debated. Bishop Lightfoot was engaged in controversy about it at the time of the Revised Version.[16] There can be little doubt that his view, which was also that of the majority of the early Fathers, is the right one, and that the word should be taken as masculine, translated "the wicked one", and referred to Satan.[17] It fits better on the whole with the use of the word elsewhere in Matthew's Gospel, as also with that in John's;[18] it gives a proper force to the word "deliver" (rescue), which is more naturally used of rescue from a personal power than from an abstraction, and it would certainly accord with our interpretation of the previous petition, with which it is so closely connected, as in Jewish thought the final crisis of trial was pictured in personal terms as a revolt against God led by the ruler of the rival kingdom of evil, Satan or his equivalent. Jesus himself thought in these terms. The kingdom of God was not for him an abstraction, but a concrete reality, waxing as the rival kingdom of evil waned, and the evidence of its waning, its defeat and retreat, he saw in the victorious works of his ministry, especially in his exorcisms.*

Here evil appears in its darkest, most iniquitous and most mysterious form, not as a debt owed to God, nor even as the temptation of men to apostasy from the root of their being, but as an independent, malignant personal power, himself wholly evil and the source of evil to others, whose existence is indeed still permitted by God, and whose ultimate destruction at God's hands is certain, but who at present comes as near as may be to disputing the world with God. The problem for our spiritual integrity here becomes most acute, for do we, and can we, believe in such a figure? This question is part of a far reaching and most difficult debate whether, and how far, we are bound by our Christian faith to the thought forms of the first century A.D. in Palestine, even if they be the thought forms of the incarnate Son of God himself, and how far we are at liberty, or are in honour bound, to decode from them some proper equivalent for them to which we can honestly assent.[19] There will be good men on both sides of this debate. It will be said that we ought not to do anything to minimize the seriousness of evil or to encourage people to think lightly of it; and who will

* Matt. 12.25–9＝Luke 11.17–22.

not agree? But it may be answered that it is precisely a quasi-belief in a spiritual being who for many a long year has been little more than a comic figure, a belief which even in those who wish to be most orthodox is often an inert and inoperative belief, which is likely to minimize the seriousness of evil. It will be said that the worst manifestations of evil are in the form of deep spiritual perversity beyond what we ordinarily know, and that it is congruent to ascribe its origin and force to a spiritual being devoted to it. But it may be replied that it is precisely the Christian Gospel, with its exalted vision of man as a being made in the divine image and for fellowship with God but capable of choosing to be God to himself, which locates the height of spiritual evil in this stature of man,[20] and that a being wholly devoted to evil is hardly congruent with anything, since as such he is beyond redemption, and there would be no reason for God to permit his continued existence, unless it were his impotence to bring it to an end. It will be said that we neglect at our peril Christian spiritual experience in the past, and the evidence which it believed itself to have of the diabolic, and our own evidence when we call anything demonic. But it may be replied that we must not be taken in either by inadequate formulations of others or by our own metaphors, and that when it comes to the acid test of encounter with serious spiritual disorder we send for the doctor, the priest, or the psychiatrist, and it has not occurred to us for many a year to send for the exorcist.[21] Questions raised for our spiritual integrity by this petition are whether belief in the devil plays any active part in our thinking and praying, or whether it is an inert belief. And if inert, do we regard it as reprehensible for ourselves or for the Church to neglect an essential truth, and would we throw ourselves enthusiastically into its recovery? Or would we prefer as an expression of the opaque mystery of iniquity the abstract word "evil", even if it be an incorrect translation?

6

The Lord's Prayer and the Lord

WHEN we have reached the end of the petitions in the Lord's Prayer, and have previously disposed of the doxology, can there be anything left to be said? Strangely, almost everything still remains to be said. The Lord's Prayer must be unique among the great prayers of the world—to give it for a moment that status—in this respect, that only for a short time can it have been prayed with the same sense as when it was delivered, and can its words have retained the meanings which they had for the disciples at the time of its delivery. We have no means of knowing how long the ministry of Jesus lasted, nor at what point in the ministry the Prayer was given, nor how often the disciples prayed it while he was still with them in the flesh, but one thing is fairly clear, that after his death and resurrection and the coming of the Holy Spirit the Prayer must have suffered a sea change for them, its emphasis altered and its words deflected in their meaning. The words of the Prayer—father, holy, name, kingdom, will, bread, forgiveness, temptation, evil— did not stand still, and they could no longer mean exactly what they had meant when the disciples had first heard the Prayer, and when the death and resurrection of Jesus and the coming of the Spirit were still future and unknown. By these things—his death and resurrection and the Spirit—the disciples now lived, and these things filled out and reshaped the words. The words so filled out and reshaped now belonged properly to Jesus in his new state, and were the means of talking principally about him as they had now come to know him. It was now impossible to repeat the Lord's Prayer simply in the sense it had had when it was given them; the process had begun, which was to continue until now, of praying the Lord's Prayer in and through the Lord and all that the Lord came to mean to them.

There is here reflected in the sphere of prayer a truth about the Christian religion from the beginning which has its own peculiar fascination. It is that Christianity is a religion of two parts, and the relation between the parts is by no means obvious, but rather one of considerable subtlety. This bi-polarity shows itself in a number of ways. One of them is the New Testament itself. In the early days of its growth and gradual formation in the second century it was sometimes spoken of as in two parts, called the Gospel and the Apostle. Under the heading of the Gospel came to be included the four individual gospels, and under the heading of the Apostle came to be included the letters supposed to come from apostles, together with Acts and Revelation. Thus Christianity was not simply what Jesus had said and done, and living by what he had said and done (the Gospel); it was also what had come about as the result of what he had said and done, and living by that (the Apostle). Contrariwise, Christianity was not simply the religious experience of Christians from Pentecost onwards (the Apostle); it was that experience related in some way to what Jesus had said and done (the Gospel).

Related in some way. But in what way? For though the Gospel and the Apostle are closely connected, they are very different from one another in shape and content, in manner and spiritual style. The Apostle is not spiritual experience in general; it revolves round the words "Jesus Christ". This does not, however, mean repeating again and again what Jesus had said; at least it does not look like that. It is possible both to overstate and to underestimate the apparent indifference of the apostles to what Jesus had said and done as guides to life, but the fact remains that in their epistles, as we have them, they very rarely settle a matter of belief or practice—which they are doing most of the time—by an appeal to what Jesus had said or done. They appeal rather to his death and resurrection, and to the illumination of the Christian mind by the Spirit. On the other side, what Jesus had said and done (the Gospel), had been said and done in particular situations in Galilee or Jerusalem, and was directed to those situations. So far as the Synoptic Gospels are concerned there is little in them by way of a blue-print in advance for that religion of the Apostle which was to emerge, the indwelling of the Christian in Christ by the Spirit in the Church. It is true that the Gospel story points forward to a future, and this is a very important truth about it. The gospels are not the record of a life and teaching which were self-contained and a rounded whole, but rather of something which was itself incomplete, and which could not be what it was except by being incomplete. As William Sanday once wrote, "I doubt if we have appreciated the preliminary and preparatory character of the Lord's mission".[1] It was preliminary and preparatory because it was to lead on to something else, but what it was to lead on to is not contained in the Gospel story itself. The relation between the two parts of Christianity, the Gospel and the Apostle, is close but it is not obvious, and heavy-handed and harmonistic attempts to make it so do not advance our understanding of either.

The Lord's Prayer provides a signal illustration of this bi-polarity. First, by its very title. Strictly speaking "The Lord's Prayer" is a misnomer, for there is no evidence that the Lord ever prayed it, and that is not how it got its name. For the Lord's Prayer in the sense of the prayer which the Lord himself prayed we have to go, apart from the short sentences uttered in Gethsemane, to something which is the very opposite of brief and succinct— the long prayer which is put into his mouth in the seventeenth chapter of John's Gospel. This prayer might be called the holy of holies in this Gospel. Throughout chapters 13–16 the Lord, his public ministry over and the world shut out, and the traitor already departed to do his work, unfolds to his own, whom he now calls his friends,* what cannot be revealed to the world, and speaks of the new order of eternal life which is to be the fruit of his death and exaltation to the Father. But finally he turns even from them, and in their presence speaks his innermost heart in an address to the Father. When this is finished nothing more is left to be said; there is only the passion and resurrection to be narrated.

Secondly, in the matter of content this bi-polarity is to be seen. By a comparison of the Lord's Prayer with the Prayer of the Lord in John 17 something can be seen of the process by which the words of the Lord's Prayer came to be filled out, and to shift their emphasis and meaning

* John 15.15.

75

as a result of the new situation brought about by the Lord's death and resurrection. It has been plausibly suggested that the Prayer of the Lord in John 17 is written around the themes of the Lord's Prayer,[2] and that it is a kind of Johannine equivalent for it, but it is also "a summary of Johannine theology relative to the work of Christ".[3] The same themes recur, but with a difference, and the difference is the result of what Christians have come to know of the Lord through his death and resurrection and the illumination of the Spirit. Thus, corresponding to "Father" in the Lord's Prayer, we have in John 17 "Father" four times, and "holy Father" and "righteous Father".* Corresponding to "Hallowed be thy name", we have "I manifested thy name", "I made known unto them thy name", "keep them in thy name", "I kept them in thy name which thou hast given me".† Corresponding to "Thy kingdom come", we have "Glorify thy Son, that the Son may glorify thee, even as thou gavest him authority over all flesh".‡ Corresponding to "Thy will be done in earth and in heaven", we have "I glorified thee on the earth, having accomplished the work which thou gavest me to do. And now, O Father, glorify thou me with thine own self with the glory which I had with thee before the world was."§ Corresponding to "Lead us not into temptation, but deliver us from the evil one", we have "I kept them in thy name: those whom thou gavest me I have kept, and none of them is lost, but the son of perdition . . . I pray . . . that thou shouldest keep them from the evil."‖ The same themes recur, but with the difference that the

* John 17.1,5,21,24,11,25.   † John 17.6,26,11,12.
‡ John 17.2.   § John 17.4f.   ‖ John 17.12–15.

fatherhood, the name, the rule of God, the deliverance from temptation and evil are now intimately associated with the person of Jesus himself, and are made sure to men because of the work of Christ, which is here spoken of in advance as already completed, and because of an unbroken unity between Father and Son, first in heaven and now on earth. This is no longer simply to pray the Lord's Prayer as taught by the Lord; it is to pray the Lord's Prayer in and through the Lord.

The separate petitions of the Lord's Prayer may now be briefly considered all over again from the new point of view. "Father." The Christianity of the Apostle is without doubt a religion of love and obedience of those who are sons towards the God who is their heavenly Father, and to a degree unprecedented in, and unprepared for by, Judaism the divine Fatherhood is a hallmark of it. The word "Father" is used of God some hundred and fifty times in the New Testament in the forms "God the Father", "Our God and Father", "The Father of our Lord Jesus Christ", "the Father" (nearly seventy of these instances are in the Fourth Gospel). It has almost become a metonym for God. How has this come about? Not simply, or even chiefly, because Jesus had placed the divine Fatherhood in the forefront of his teaching, had spoken constantly about it, and the apostles are simply echoing him. We have seen reason to believe that Jesus spoke about it a good deal less often than the Synoptic Gospels, especially Matthew's, allow us to suppose. Nor because he himself used, and taught others to use, the extraordinarily intimate address "Abba" to God, though this may have been important. Nor because he had joined with the disciples in a common address to God of this kind. Such evidence as we have suggests that Jesus did not include himself alongside his disciples in a common address to God as the common Father, but that he distinguished himself from them. They are to become sons of one who is called "your Father" by reproducing the character of the Father; there is no sign that he thought of himself in this way. He was already the Son of the Father. According to John this distinction was maintained even in the one passage where he is recorded as calling them his brethren—"Go to my brethren, and say unto them, I ascend unto my Father, and your Father; and to my God and your God."*

What did produce the intense conviction in the early Church that God is Father was not what Jesus had said, but what he was, and what he was now known to be through his death and resurrection and the illumination of the Spirit—the Son. Father and son are correlatives. They exist for each other, and cannot be fully grasped without each other. A fullness of fatherhood can only be conveyed if there is a fullness of sonship through which to convey it. Already in the Synoptic Gospels this peeps through the crucial and highly theological incidents of the Baptism and Transfiguration. They are crucial because from them streams the light by which the rest of the story of the earthly life of Jesus is intended to be seen. They are highly theological and symbolic because by means of a heavenly voice Jesus is hailed by God himself as the beloved (only) Son. This is taken further as a result of his death and resurrection, for his death is understood as the proving and sealing of his love and obedience as the Son of the Father, and his resurrection is the Father's acknow-

* John 20.17. Cf. Matt. 26.29; 25.34; Luke 22.29.

78

ledgement of him as Son, no longer in heavenly and symbolic voice, but by the act of raising him from death. Hence for Paul the sonship of Christians is their adoption by God, which has been made possible by the sending of him who is the Son into the world, and it is through receiving the spirit of his sonship, that is, his very inner character, that they are able to reproduce his obedience, and to cry along with him "Abba, Father".* Jesus as Son has moved into the centre of the picture, and the divine Fatherhood is grasped through what he is. The fourth evangelist takes this to its conclusion, and rewrites the earthly story of Jesus with this as the master key, so that his gospel is an extended exposition of the mutual thought and action of the Father and the Son. From then onwards, to pray "Our Father" is to pray the Lord's Prayer through, and in union with, the Lord.

"Hallowed be thy name." The name of God, his nature as revealed, and the hallowing of his name, his making himself to be acknowledged for the God he is, which were so characteristic of Judaism and are yet confined in the Synoptic Gospels to this petition in the Lord's Prayer, do not become more frequent in the New Testament. It remains almost silent about God's name, except that in what may be his equivalent for the temptation in Gethsemane John records that Jesus prayed, "Father, glorify thy name",† as he also records as words of Jesus that he has come into the world, and does his work in the world, in his Father's name,‡ and, in the prayer of chapter 17, that he has manifested to the disciples God's name, and has kept them in it.§ Again, Jesus moves into the centre as

* Gal. 4.4–7.   † John 12.28.   ‡ John 5.43; 10.25.
§ John 17.6,11f,26.

79

the custodian of the name of God. What is more remarkable is that the name of Jesus becomes as frequent as the name of God is infrequent. Almost, but not quite, it takes the place of the name of God. The prerogatives of God pass to him; the benefits of salvation are through him. Men begin their new life by baptism into his name,* that is, into his possession and control; they are justified, that is, put right with God, and receive the gift of the last days, the forgiveness of sins, and life through his name;† they believe in his name, that is, put in him a total trust which properly is given to God;‡ they call upon his name, that is, in worship, which belongs only to God.§ They perform the works of salvation, preach, teach, rebuke, exhort, condemn, heal, exorcise, and pray in his name.‖ They suffer and die for his name.¶ This is possible only because his name, which here as elsewhere in the Bible denotes his character and nature, is no longer simply Jesus, the rabbi and prophet of Nazareth, who is asked by his personal adherents to be taught to pray as John, another prophet, had taught his own, but Jesus, the Christ and the Lord. "God hath made him both Lord and Christ, this Jesus . . ."** When Paul, in what is thought by many to be an early Christian hymn, says that because of the descent of Jesus into the flesh, and the obedience involved in it, God has exalted him and given him the name which is

* Acts 2.38; 8.16; 10.48; 19.5.
† 1 Cor. 6.11; Luke 24.47; Acts 2.38, 10.43; John 20.31.
‡ John 1.12; Acts 3.16; 1 John 3.23; 5.13.
§ Acts 9.14,21; 22.16; Rom. 10.13f; 1 Cor. 1.2.
‖ Acts 3.6; 4.7–12; 5.28,40; 8.12; 9.27ff; 16.18; 1 Cor. 1.10; 5.4; Col. 3.17; 2 Thess. 3.6.
¶ Acts 5.41; 15.26; 21.13; 1 Pet. 4.14.
** Acts 2.36.

above every name, so that at the name of Jesus every knee should bow and every tongue confess, he is applying to Jesus, the erstwhile prophet and teacher, what Isaiah had applied to God. The name above every name is the name *Kyrios*, Lord, as the concluding words show—"every tongue should confess that Jesus Christ is Lord, to the glory of God the Father",* and *Kyrios*, Lord, is in the Old Testament the name of God, or rather the substitute for it, since it was too holy to pronounce. The name, or person, of God as Father is made known through the name, or person, of Jesus as Son, because they are one in nature and will, and "he that has seen me has seen the Father".⁴ The prayer of the Lord in John 17 is, therefore, no longer a petition to God to hallow his name. That has already been done, for "I manifested thy name unto the men whom thou gavest me ... while I was with them I kept them in thy name. . . . I made known unto them thy name." It is now a petition that what Jesus has effectually done will continue: "Holy Father, keep them in thy name [i.e. as thy possession] which thou hast given me, that they may be one, even as we are."† This is no longer simply to pray the Lord's Prayer as the Lord once taught, but to pray through it for a continuation of the union with God and the unity in God which the Lord has made available.

"Thy kingdom come." Here there is a remarkable sea change. In the Synoptic Gospels the term "the kingdom of God" is ubiquitous, present in all their sources and in different kinds of sayings and the subject of all kinds of statements. It is a ruling concept through which Jesus says a great deal of what he has to say about the demands of

* Phil. 2.5–11; Isa. 45.23.   † John 17.6,12,26,11.

God and the imminence of his salvation. It is not the term through which the apostles say what they have to say. In the rest of the New Testament it has moved on to the circumference and has become somewhat conventional. In Acts it is used six times in formal phrases such as "preaching" or "attesting the kingdom of God".* In Paul's epistles it is used ten times, generally in somewhat conventional statements that persons of such and such a kind shall not enter the kingdom of God.† In the Johannine writings it has disappeared altogether except for an isolated reference in John's Gospel. There is one reference in Revelation, and that is all.‡ What has happened? Have the apostolic writers deserted the gospel of Jesus for another? No, rather they have come to see it from the other side of his death and resurrection, when what he had initiated had come to completion, and he with it.

Even in his lifetime Jesus had not spoken of the kingdom in the abstract as an entity or future possibility. He had proclaimed it as being at the doors, and as linked with what he was doing and saying. He could even say that in some sense it had arrived, even if in hidden form. Looking back across his death and resurrection the apostles came to see how little and how much it had come with him. How little, because God rules completely in his will and heart alone; how much, because God rules there completely. So their attention was fixed less on the kingdom than on him. Whereas the Jews had read off from their conceptions of the kingdom their conception of the king in that kingdom, for the apostles it was, through the

* Acts 1.3; 8.12; 14.22; 19.8; 20.25; 28.23,31.
† Rom. 14.17; 1 Cor. 4.20; 6.9f; 15.50; Gal. 5.21; Col. 4.11; 2 Thess. 1.5 (Eph. 5.5; 1 Thess. 2.12).   ‡ John 3.3,5; Rev. 12.10.

impact of Jesus, the other way round. They read off the nature of the kingdom from him in whom it was embodied.[5] As they had transferred the name from God to Jesus, so they transferred the kingdom, and could speak of God having already translated them into the kingdom of the Son of his love, where he reigns until all enemies are put down, when he will hand over the kingdom to the Father.* The Fourth Gospel again illustrates the change, for while the kingdom of God has disappeared altogether from the teaching of Jesus except for the isolated mention in the conversation with Nicodemus, the story of the passion in this gospel is dominated by the theme of Jesus as king. He is king not only of the Jews, who protest that they have no king but Caesar, but king of men, in a kingdom which he now calls "my kingdom", king in the kingdom of truth, and his passion demonstrates his royalty.†

The double title for God current in Judaism, "our Father, our King", would seem to have been split into two by the Christian Gospel, each part now developing on its own. The first develops with the deepening apprehension of God as Father, the second with the virtual disappearance of the title "King" for God and its monopoly by Jesus in the form of Lord. The expectancy and urgency which belonged to Jesus' own Gospel does not disappear in the Gospel of the apostles, but it is attached no longer, as with him, to the kingdom of God, but to the person of the Lord, the King. Life is to be lived under the shadow of the Lord's coming. The command "be not anxious", which in the teaching of Jesus is grounded in the con-

* Col. 1.13; 1 Cor. 15.25–8.
† John 12.12–19; 18.33–40; 19.1–5, 12–16, 19–22.

fidence that the Father in his providential care will give all that is needful to those who seek first God's kingdom, is in Paul, together with the joy and assurance which go with it, grounded in the conviction that "the Lord is at hand".★ As the closing words of his First Epistle to the Corinthians Paul reproduces, still in its primitive Aramaic dress, the cry of the early Church *Maran-atha*, "our Lord come",† and the New Testament closes with the words, "Yea: I come quickly. Amen: come, Lord Jesus."‡

The third petition in Matthew's version of the Lord's Prayer was seen to be essentially the same petition as the second, but to add with the word "will" a more inward and ethical note to the kingdom. So also the titles Christ, King, Lord are somewhat official designations of authority and status. If one asks of the apostolic writers what was the inward quality through which Jesus qualifies to be their sole bearer, they reply unanimously that it was his sonship, his obedience, his performance of the will of the Father. That this is the clue to his life is indicated in his Baptism and Transfiguration with the words of the voice: "Thou art [This is] my beloved Son, in thee I am well pleased [hear ye him]."§ That it is the clue to his death, and invests that death with the quality of the sacrifice inaugurating the new covenant between God and men, is indicated in the prayer in Gethsemane: "Abba, Father . . . not what I will, but what thou wilt." ‖ Paul can sum up in the one word "obedience" the relation of Jesus to the Father, which undoes the disobedience of Adam which had perverted the world.¶ The author of Hebrews sees in

★ Phil. 4.5f.   † 1 Cor. 16.22.   ‡ Rev. 22.20.
§ Mark 1.11; 9.7.   ‖ Mark 14.36.   ¶ Rom. 5.19; Phil. 2.8.

the obedience of his will as Son the clue to his life of temptation and suffering, as also the inner meaning of his death, which makes of it the one and only sacrifice, procuring our sanctification and cleansing even the heavenly places themselves.* In the hymn already alluded to the lordship of Jesus over the universe is conferred on him in virtue of his obedience to death, the death of the cross.† The true interests of the world, which are God's interests in it, are secure in his hands, because his will is one with that of the heavenly Father. Once more the prayer of the Lord in John 17 offers the commentary. The equivalent of the petition "Thy kingdom come" is "O Father, glorify thou me with thine own self with the glory which I had with thee before the world was", and this petition can be made because it can be said of the Son "thou gavest him authority over all flesh", and the basis of both is not a prayer but the statement, "I glorified thee on the earth, having accomplished the work which thou hast given me to do".‡ The Lord's Prayer is now prayed in the light of the finished work of the Lord whose prayer it was.

"Give us to-day to-morrow's bread." The words in John 17, "that whatsoever thou hast given him, to them he should give eternal life", are an echo of earlier words in the sixth chapter of John's Gospel: "I am come down from heaven, not to do mine own will, but the will of him that sent me. And this is the will of him that sent me, that of all which he hath given me I should lose nothing, but should raise it up at the last day."§ Jesus spans heaven and earth by his obedience to the will of the Father, and so is able to

* Heb. 5.8; 10.7–10; 9.23–8.   † Phil. 2.9 "Wherefore . . .".
‡ John 17.5,2,4.   § John 6.37–40.

give men eternal life, the life of heaven on earth. But in this sixth chapter eternal life, a synonym for the kingdom of God, which is to be a present possession of the disciple and a pledge of his final resurrection, is spoken of as bread, as the bread of life or living bread. This is not simply the bread which Jesus gives, but which he himself is, and they who eat of him will not die but live eternally.* Bread also is a word which Jesus has here captured and annexed to himself, and once this has happened the petition, "Give us to-day our *epiousian* bread", cannot be uttered without the thought of it.

Finally, the difference between the Gospel which Jesus preached and the Gospel which the apostles preached about him is nowhere more evident than in the matter of sin and forgiveness, temptation and evil. Jesus did not theorize on sin and the necessity of atonement, on temptation and its source, on evil and its origin. He is no theologian. He speaks directly of the readiness of the Father to forgive on repentance, as in the parable of the prodigal son. He makes men aware of it by keeping as close as possible to those who were most in need of it, and on occasion he confers it with divine authority.† He commands his disciples to pray to be preserved from the great trial, though he has submitted to it and emerged unscathed, and is working in the power of his victory over it. He knows his life to be a conflict with a rival kingdom of evil, against which he wages constant warfare, seeing in his mighty acts, especially his successful exorcisms and those of his disciples, tokens that this rival kingdom is broken and its ruler deposed. But as yet all is

* John 6.32–58.
† Luke 15.11ff; Mark 2.15=Luke 15.1; Mark 2.5; Luke 7.48.

inconclusive, and the issues of his life and work are still wide open. He speaks of a fire still to be lit and of a baptism still to be undergone, through which he and his work will reach their destined completion.* There was a force of temptation still to be endured which only he could endure, and an onslaught to be met when evil would put forth all its power, and he set his face to go to Jerusalem, repeating that the Son of Man must be rejected, suffer, and be killed, and that it was the divine will that it should be so.† And there it is left.

The apostolic writers, however, are theologians, and are compelled to be so. They are full of the ideas of sin and atonement, of reconciliation and sacrifice, of justification and grace, for they now look upon sin, temptation, and evil through his death, in which the issues of his life had come to a head, and they see in his death something by which the breach between men and God was immeasurably widened before ever it was closed, and by which the full ravages of evil in God's world were exposed before ever they were healed. The death of the obedient Son of God and of the Son of Man, the lord of the world, at the hands of the world, unveils a schism running from top to bottom of the world. The gracious free gift of forgiveness, the cancellation of all debts, can now be thought of only in relation to a death which pays the debt and writes off what was written against us.‡ The bold approach to God, and fellowship with God, are realities through a temptation which is without sin, and a self-offering which is all that sacrifice wanted to be.§ The glorious liberty of the children of God is the fruit

* Luke 12.49f; Mark 10.39.   † Mark 8.31f; 9.31; 10.32ff.
‡ Col. 2.13ff; 2 Cor. 5.18–21.   § Heb. 4.15; 10.5–18.

of a destruction of evil which is valid for all time, and of an expulsion of Satan, the prince of this world, who falls back defeated because there is nothing in Jesus for him to get hold of.* The petitions, therefore, in John 17 are no longer "Cancel us our debts, as we remit to our debtors" and "Lead us not into temptation but deliver us from the evil one", but that the Father himself will preserve the disciples in that same state of safety in which Jesus had preserved them by his presence with them, and that he will maintain them as they are now, intact from the evil one, and consecrated to God in the truth by virtue of his own consecration of himself as a sacrifice on their behalf. Only the mystery of iniquity leaves its traces even here, for there is an exception; the son of perdition has been lost.†

Christianity is in two parts, and the relation between them is subtle. The continuity between them is provided by the continuance of Jesus himself, who is the subject of both parts, first as rabbi, teacher, and prophet, and then as messiah, lord, and head of his body. The Lord's Prayer bears the marks of the time of its first delivery, when the issues of Jesus' life, and therefore of human life, had not yet come to a head. Perhaps not long afterwards they came to a head in the crucial events of which Holy Week and Easter are the memorial, and from that time onwards disciples were no longer able to pray the Lord's Prayer as they had first prayed it, but only in and through the Lord. Only in this way have Christians ever been able to pray it since. What works the sea change is that Jesus moves into the centre, and all the things of God are apprehended through him. For all that, he never dis-

* John 12.31; 14.30; 16.11.　　　† John 17.11–19.

places the Father. He is never called the Father, nor is he equated with God outright. The Father always stands behind him, and what he does and is, is what it is because it is to the glory of God.* So the doxology must be allowed to come back into its own. All things are of God and to God, and his is the kingdom, the power and the glory, for ever. Amen. The Lord's Prayer, like all Christian prayer, is in the last analysis prayed in the Spirit through Christ to the Father.

* Phil. 2.10f; John 17.4.

Notes

CHAPTER 1

1 *De Oratione*, i. The translation is from E. Evans, *Tertullian's Tract on the Prayer*, the Latin text with critical notes, and English translation, an introduction and explanatory notes (1953). Compendious brevity is noted as a mark of the Prayer by others. St Cyprian, who in his commentary often depends on his "master" Tertullian, says (ch. 28): "What wonder, dearly beloved brethren, if the prayer which God taught us is of such character, for by his teaching he abridged all our prayer in wholesome language? This had already been foretold by the prophet Isaiah, when full of the Holy Spirit, he spoke of the majesty and kindness of God. A word that sums up, he says, and abridges in righteousness, since God will make an abridged speech throughout the world" (Isa. 10.22f LXX). (Translation by H. Gee, *St Cyprian on the Lord's Prayer*, 1904.) Cf. also St Augustine, in Letter 130 to the Roman widow, Proba, in reply to her request for instruction on prayer: "And if you go over all the words of holy prayers, you will, I believe, find nothing which cannot be comprised and summed up in the petitions of the Lord's Prayer" (*The Works of Aurelius Augustine*, ed. M. Dods, vol. 13, p. 159). It raises the question whether the brevity of much of the teaching in the gospels is solely due to the form taken by the gospel tradition in the course of transmission, or whether it was also a characteristic of Jesus. Certainly the Lord's Prayer is brief compared with liturgical prayer, which tends to prolixity, and, in general, with contemporary Jewish prayers. "Later liturgical prose develops in the direction of an increasingly rhetorical form . . . such rhetoric is wholly absent from the prayers of the *Didache*,

and the Roman Anaphora of Hippolytus, as from the Paternoster" (A. Baumstark, *Comparative Liturgy*, 1958, p. 61).

2 Ibid., i.

3 It is noteworthy that both Mark and John can give an account of the life and teaching of Jesus without referring to the Prayer (but on John see further ch. 6). Little can be argued from the silence of the rest of the New Testament, since what a writer of an epistle will or will not mention depends on the situation to which he is writing. As has often been pointed out we would have no reference to the Eucharist in the Pauline epistles had not some of the Corinthians come to it drunk (1 Cor. 11.17–34). There may be references to the Prayer in Rom. 8.15 and Gal. 4.6, but this is not certain.

4 This context is clearly artificial, since the Prayer can hardly have been given primarily as an example of brevity in prayer, without regard to its content. In practice the Church, in defiance of this context, has been most repetitious in its use of the Lord's Prayer.

5 As, for example, in Morning and Evening Prayer and the Communion in the course of a single service.

6 Origen, Περὶ Εὐχῆς, xviii,2–3. See E. G. Jay, *Origen's Treatise on Prayer*. Translation and Notes with an account of the practice and doctrine of prayer from New Testament times to Origen (1954).

7 As when one harmonist had Jairus's daughter raised from the dead three times, because of the three slightly divergent accounts in the gospels.

8 For a discussion of the origin of the doxology, F. H. Chase, *The Lord's Prayer in the Early Church. Texts and Studies*, ed. J. A. Robinson, vol. 1, no. 3, 1891, pp. 168ff.

9 *Didache* 8.

10 Origen, op. cit., xviii, p. 2.

11 This is the analysis of E. Lohmeyer, *Das Vater-unser* (Göttingen, 4th ed., 1960), pp. 14f. Cf. also J. Jeremias, "The Lord's Prayer in Modern Research" (*Expository Times*, vol. 71, 1959–60, pp. 141ff).

12 Lohmeyer, op. cit., p. 15.

13 C. F. Burney, *The Poetry of our Lord* (1925), p. 113.

14 Lohmeyer, op. cit., p. 16. K. G. Kuhn, *Achtzehngebet und Vaterunser und der Reim* (Tübingen 1950), pp. 38ff, considers that both

Matthew's and Luke's versions, when turned back into Aramaic, exhibit not only rhythm but rhyme like the Jewish prayer, the *Eighteen Benedictions*.

15 So G. Dalman, *The Words of Jesus* (1902), p. 189.

16 Which is the order in 1 Cor. 10.16 (though not that in 11.24f) and in *Didache* 9.

17 In *Didache* 9 there are no sacrificial words accompanying the cup, and the bread is associated with the gathering of the Church into the kingdom.

18 On the small number of authentic references of Jesus to the Holy Spirit, see C. K. Barrett, *The Holy Spirit and the Gospel Tradition* (1947).

CHAPTER 2

1 See Kittel's *Theologisches Wörterbuch zum Neuen Testament*, ed. G. Friedrich (Stuttgart), vol. 5, pp. 948ff, for "Father" in ancient religion.

2 Origen, op. cit., xxii: "It is worth a very careful search into the Old Testament, as men call it, to see if it is possible anywhere to find therein a prayer of anybody who addresses God as Father. For up to the present, although I have searched according to my ability, I have not found one. I do not say that God is not spoken of as a Father, or that those who are thought to believe in God are not called sons of God, but that I have not yet found in a prayer that boldness of speech (mentioned by the Saviour) in calling God "Father" (Jay, op. cit., pp. 144f). Augustine (*De Sermone Domini in Monte secudum Matthaeum*, 15): "For many things are said in praise of God, which, being scattered variously and widely over all the Holy Scriptures, every one will be able to consider when he reads them: yet nowhere is there found a precept for the people of Israel, that they should say 'Our Father', or that they should pray to God as Father; but as Lord He was made known to them, as being yet servants, i.e. still living according to the flesh" (Translation in *The Nicene and Post-Nicene Fathers*, vol. 6, 38f).

3 Johs. Pedersen, *Israel* (1926), I–II, pp. 46ff.

4 Kittel's *Wörterbuch*, vol. 5, pp. 970f.

5 The text of this prayer, also called *Amidah*, can be most conveniently studied in the appendix to C. W. Dugmore's *The*

Influence of the Synagogue upon the Divine Office (1944), pp. 114ff, where the Hebrew text and English translation are set out in parallel columns of both the traditional text of the whole *Eighteen Benedictions* (the Babylonian *Amidah*) and of an earlier Palestinian *Amidah* recoverable from fragments discovered in a Cairo Genizah and closer to the form current in the time of Jesus. Benediction 4 in the Palestinian version begins: "O favour us, our Father . . .", and Benediction 6 in both versions begins: "Forgive us, our Father . . . .".

6 The evidence is examined in detail by H. F. D. Sparks, "The Doctrine of the Divine Fatherhood in the Gospels" (in *Studies in the Gospels*, ed. D. E. Nineham, 1955), who concludes that: (i) "if we are to trust the evidence Jesus will have spoken of God as Father less often than a casual reading of the gospels might suggest, and certainly far less often than is popularly supposed"; and (ii) "the total picture presented . . . is the same throughout—God, in the first place, is the Father of Jesus because Jesus is the Messianic Son, but, in the second place, He is also Father of those who follow Jesus, who have perceived and acknowledged his Messianic status, and who are, in consequence, members of the Messianic (or Christian) community" (pp. 259f). So also, Dalman, op. cit., p. 190. This is challenged by H. W. Montefiore, "God as Father in the Synoptic Gospels" (*New Testament Studies*, vol. 3, no. 1, November 1956, pp. 31ff), who argues that the evidence shows that God's Fatherhood of all men underlies the teaching of Jesus and is at times expressed in it. The question frequently turns upon the evaluation of the context and audience provided for a saying by the evangelists. Are sayings such as "Your heavenly Father knoweth that ye have need of all these things" (Matt. 6.32) or "Are not two sparrows sold for a farthing? and not one of them shall fall to the ground without your Father" (Matt. 10.29), to be taken as spoken only to the immediate audience of disciples, or also to a further audience, actual or implied, in the background? And whichever way the question is answered, has the evangelist rightly interpreted the force of the saying in providing it with this context? In view of the nature of the gospel material, which came to the evangelist without context, these are questions which are not easily answered.

7 Mark 14.36; 13.32; 11.25. On the doubtfulness of the last see Sparks, op. cit., pp. 243f.

8 As perhaps, in 12.24, compared with Matt. 6.26, since Luke 12.30 has it (though 12.28 and Matt. 6.30 both have "God" and not "Father").

9 Rom. 8.15; Gal. 4.6. The verb "cry out" may imply some special circumstance, and not simply the recitation of the Lord's Prayer. The double 'Aββᾶ ὁ πατήρ is, however, something of a puzzle, as can be seen from the difficulty of knowing how to translate it. (See S. V. McCasland, *Journal of Biblical Literature*, vol. 72, 1953, pp. 79ff.) As it stands the text should be translated into English, "Father, Father" or, "O Father, O Father", since Abba and ὁ πατήρ mean the same, but this is absurd. As Paul is writing in Greek for Greek readers why does he not write simply ὁ πατήρ? If he adds Abba because it is a hallowed survival from the time when Christians still confessed their faith in Aramaic, why does he not write Abba by itself, as in 1 Cor. 16.22 he reproduces *Maran-atha* without explanation? If the two together are meant to reproduce alternative cries in a bilingual Church, why is it not indicated that the second is a translation of the first? Mark 14.36 is even more curious, since elsewhere when Mark introduces an Aramaic word from the tradition he adds the Greek equivalent for his readers with the words "which is (being interpreted)", as in 3.17; 5.41; 7.11,34; 15.22,34 (cf. Matt. 1.23; Acts 1.19; John 5.2; 9.7; 19.13,17). Why does he not do so here, if ὁ πατήρ is meant to be an equivalent of Abba, and his readers are not to suppose that Jesus said two things, Abba and ὁ πατήρ. It is these considerations which led McCasland to argue that Abba had become a metonym for "God" (cf. Mal. 2.10; Wisd. 14.3; 3 Macc. 6.4,8) and that Abba, ὁ πατήρ lies behind such New Testament expressions as "God the Father" (1 Thess. 1.1), "God our Father" (2 Thess. 1.1f; Phil. 1.2; Philem. 3), and "Our God and Father" (1 Thess. 1.3; 3.11,13; Phil. 4.20). This would seem to depend, however, on taking Abba as Ab with the definite article added to give it the determinate form, "the father", whereas Dalman, Jeremias, and others maintain that it is a vocative form by contraction from Abbai, "father".

10 In "Kennzeichen der ipsissima vox Jesu" (in *Synoptische Studien*,

94

A. Wikenhauser zum 70. Geburtstag, München 1953, pp. 87ff), and elsewhere. Perhaps too much weight should not be put on this, as the teaching and practice of few rabbis were so elaborately documented as those of the "rabbi" Jesus came to be in the gospels. Jeremias quotes a partial exception in the incident of Hanan, the grandson of Onias, which belongs to the last years of the first century B.C., when he was asked by children in a time of drought to give them rain, and prayed: "Ruler of the world, do it for the sake of these, who cannot yet distinguish between an abba who can give rain and an abba who can give no rain" (*Ta'anit* 23b). The author of the article on Abba in the Jewish Encyclopaedia quotes in addition the rebuke of Simon ben Shetah to Onias: "I would excommunicate thee for thine irreverent mode of prayer were it not that before God thou art a privileged son, who sayeth to his father 'Abba, do this, or do that for me', and the father granteth him whatever he wisheth" (*Ta'anit* 23a), though this hardly seems sufficient for his judgement that Abba "was the formula for addressing God most familiar to Jewish saints of the New Testament times". It should be observed that the diminutive element, and the element of familiarity in Abba, are largely lost when it is rendered, as in the New Testament, by πατήρ, the ordinary word for "father".

11 See L. Hodgson, *For Faith and Freedom* (1957), vol. 2, ch. 8, "Providence and Prayer".

12 Kittel's *Wörterbuch*, vol. 5, p. 997.

13 B. L. Gildersleeve, quoted in J. H. Moulton, *A Grammar of New Testament Greek*, p. 173.

14 "We are God's fellow-workers" (1 Cor. 3.9) does not mean that Paul and Barnabas are fellow-workers with God, but that they are fellow-workers with each other, and that both together are God's possession.

15 Except in Old Testament quotations (Matt. 21.9 and parallels) and a hymn based on the Old Testament (Luke 1.49).

16 N. H. Snaith, *The Distinctive Ideas of the Old Testament* (1944), ch. 2, "The Holiness of God".

17 G. F. Moore, *Judaism* (Harvard University Press 1927), vol. 2, pp. 101f.

[18] Ibid., p. 101.

[19] The juxtaposition is weakened in Matthew's version by being compressed within the address itself—"Our Father, the [Father] in heaven". The exalted Father is to be apprehended through earthly fatherhood, but never to be confused with it. Origen comments here (op. cit., xxiii): "But when it is said that the Father of the saints is in heaven, we must not understand him to be circumscribed and to dwell in heaven in bodily fashion; for God contained in this way will then be found less than heaven if heaven contains him. We must believe that all things are contained and held together by him, by the ineffable power of his Godhead. And in general we must interpret those passages which, in so far as they are taken literally, are thought by the more simple to assert that God is in a place, in conformity with large and spiritual ideas about God" (Jay, op. cit., p. 148).

CHAPTER 3

[1] Benediction 5 (Babylonian recension): "Cause us to return, O our Father, unto thy Torah; bring us near, our King, to thy service". "Our Father, our King" occurs frequently in the New Year Prayer.

[2] Note the combination of "holy" and "all-ruler" in Rev. 4.8.

[3] L. Köhler takes kingship and lordship as the central theme of his Theologie des Alten Testaments (1936).

[4] On the Israelite conception of kingship see Johs. Pedersen, op. cit., III–IV (1940), pp. 33–106.

[5] Pss. 47; 22.28; Jer. 10.6–10; Ex. 15.18; Ps. 146.10. "King of the world" is found in Jewish prayers.

[6] See K. G. Kühn, op. cit., pp. 40ff.

[7] Benediction 11: "Restore our judges as at the first, and our counsellors as at the beginning; and reign Thou over us, Thou alone. Blessed art Thou, O Lord, who lovest judgement."

[8] Mark 9.1; Luke 22.18; Matt. 5.3,10 where the present tense is to be interpreted in the light of the future tense in the rest of the beatitudes. See W. G. Kümmel, Promise and Fulfilment (1957), ch. 1 for a full discussion of the evidence.

9 Matt. 12.28=Luke 11.20; Matt. 11.12=Luke 16.16. Kümmel, op. cit., ch. 3 for the presence of the kingdom of God, and the whole book for an account and illustration of the debate.

10 As in John's Gospel, where "eternal life", that is, the life of the coming age (the kingdom of God), has become the present possession of the Christian believer, and the future consummation has dropped into the background, and in Paul's writings, where the expectation of the coming (*parousia*) of Christ still remains but the emphasis is upon the Christian's being already "in Christ", united to Christ's death and resurrection life (Rom. 6.3–9), already risen with him and translated into the kingdom of Christ (Col. 3.1; 1.13). The answer of 2 Pet. 3.8–13 that the day of the Lord will still come as a thief, but that with the Lord a day may be a thousand years, and its delay is to give time for repentance, is an example of the acuteness of the problem and of an unsatisfactory traditional solution of it.

11 Matt. 6.1–18. "In these passages the decisive requirement is the same: the good which is to be done is to be done *completely*. He who does it partially, with reservations, just enough to fulfil the outward regulation, has not done it at all. He who refrains from murder but does not master anger has not understood that he must decide completely. He who indeed avoids adultery, but keeps lust in his heart, has not understood the prohibition of adultery, which requires of him complete purity. He who refrains simply from perjury has not seen that absolute truthfulness is demanded. . . . Jesus then sees the act as expressing the *whole* man, that is, he sees his action from the viewpoint of decision: Either–Or. Every half-way is an abomination. . . . This really means that *Jesus teaches no ethics at all* in the sense of an intelligible theory valid for all men concerning what should be done and left undone. . . . The decision is an absolute Either–Or; the good which is here required is not a relative good, which on a higher level of development can be replaced by something better—it is the will of God." (R. Bultmann, *Jesus and the Word*, 1935, pp. 90ff, 84f.)

12 The absence of this petition in Luke's version, and its close similarity with the Lord's own petition in its Matthean form (Matt. 26.42 compared with Mark 14.36=Luke 22.42, cf. also Acts 21.14), has

led to the supposition that it is a later addition (see I. Abrahams *Studies in Pharisaism and the Gospels*, 1924; 2nd series, pp. 100ff). Tertullian has the petitions concerning the kingdom and the will in the reverse order (*De Or.* 4–5), and argues that the petition on the kingdom follows that on the will because it depends upon it. This appears to show that there was still some fluidity in the text of the Prayer in Tertullian's day. In Luke's version a curious reading, "Let thy Holy Spirit come upon us and cleanse us", is read in place of "Thy kingdom come" in two manuscripts, and by Marcion, Gregory of Nyssa, and Maximus. It has been held by some that this is a genuine reading which was driven out by harmonization, but it is poorly attested, and should probably be regarded as erratic and as an adaptation, perhaps for use at baptism.

13 Some manuscripts of St Cyprian, have "sicut in coelo et in terra" ("as in heaven, so on earth"), but the principal manuscripts and Tertullian have "in coelo [caelis] et in terra" ("in heaven and in earth"), and St Augustine quotes this form as the more usual in his time.

14 Cf. "his kingdom, and his righteousness" (Matt. 6.33).

CHAPTER 4

1 In some Jewish prayers composed of short sentences it would seem that each petition was intended to be treated on its own rather than as a constituent of a whole.

2 Quoted in I. Abrahams, op. cit., p. 98, where the question of the pattern of the Prayer, and of its relation to rabbinic models, is discussed, and reference is made to other discussions of the question.

3 Benediction 9 (Palestinian recension, in Dugmore's translation): "Bless for us, O Lord our God, this year for [our] welfare, with every kind of the produce thereof, and bring near speedily the year of the end of our redemption; and give dew and rain upon the face of the earth and satisfy the world from the treasuries of Thy goodness, and do Thou give a blessing upon the work of our hands. Blessed art Thou, O Lord, who blessest the years."

4 Op. cit., xxvii, 1–7 (Jay, op. cit.).

5 See Kittel's *Wörterbuch*, vol. 2, p. 594, and also the whole article for a discussion of the problem and literature upon it.

6 See Lohmeyer, op. cit., p. 98.

7 *On a Fresh Revision of the New Testament* (1872), pp. 195ff.

8 It should be remembered that for the Jews the day began with sunset.

9 Cf. Prov. 30.8: "Give me neither poverty nor riches; feed me with food needful [sufficient] for me", and Jas. 2.15: "If a brother or sister be naked, and in lack of daily food" (τῆς ἐφημέρου τροφῆς sufficient for the day).

10 Though one of his arguments, namely, that if derived from ἐπί and εἶναι it would have been *epousios* through elision of "i", is not as strong as he thought it was, since the rule of elision is now known not to have applied as strictly in later hellenistic Greek as in classical Greek.

11 See Chase, op. cit., pp. 42ff, on the readings of the versions.

12 It is not certain that "*mahar*" in the Gospel according to the Hebrews is a re-translation back into Aramaic of ἐπιούσιος in Matthew's Gospel. It could be that the translator at this point simply reproduced the Lord's Prayer in Aramaic as he knew it.

13 Tertullian observes that the meaning of this petition is bound up with the question of the pattern of the Prayer as a whole. "But gracefully has the divine wisdom drawn up the order of the prayer, that after heavenly things, that is, after God's name, God's will, and God's kingdom, it should make place for petition for earthly necessities too: for the Lord had also stated the principle, *Seek ye first the kingdom and then even these things will be added unto you*. And yet we prefer the spiritual understanding of Give us to-day our daily bread, for Christ is our bread . . ." (*De Or.* 6, Evans's translation).

14 This rendering is placed in the margin in the New English Bible. It is adopted by J. Jeremias in "The Lord's Prayer in Modern Research" (*Expository Times*, vol. 71, 1959–60), p. 145.

15 Ex. 16.4, "I will rain bread from heaven for you"; 16.15; "It is the bread which the Lord hath given you to eat"; Neh. 9.15, "bread from heaven"; Ps. 105.40, "bread of heaven"; Ps. 78.24, "corn of heaven"; Ps. 78.25=Wisd. 16.20, "angel's food". C. Taylor (*Sayings of the Jewish Fathers*, p. 139) considered that these allusions

made it "probable that the Lord's Prayer also should have some reference to the giving of the manna".

16 Ex. 16.29. In 16.5, for "it shall be twice as much as they gather daily", the Septuagint for "daily" has the rather curious phrase τὸ καθ' ἡμέραν εἰς ἡμέραν, which may have influenced the Lukan version of this petition.

17 2 Baruch (c. A.D. 100) 29.8 has: "And it shall come to pass at that self-same time that the treasury of manna shall again descend from on high, and they will eat of it in those years, because these are they who have come to the consummation of the time." There are other rabbinic references which are later such as, "Ye shall not find it [the manna] in this age, but ye shall find it in the age that is coming" (Mekilta on Ex. 16.25), and "What did the first redeemer? He brought down the manna. And the last redeemer will bring down the manna" (Rabba Eccles. 1.9). For further references see A. Schlatter, Der Evangelist Johannes (1948), pp. 172f. A list of those who interpret this petition in the Lord's Prayer of the coming age and its feast is given under ἐπιούσιος 4.d. in W. Bauer, A Greek–English Lexicon of the New Testament, English trans. by W. F. Arndt and F. W. Gingrich (1957), and Kümmel, op. cit., p. 52, n. 104.

18 John 6.33–40: "The bread of God is that which cometh down out of heaven, and giveth life unto the world. They said therefore unto him, Lord, evermore give us this bread [πάντοτε δὸς ἡμῖν τὸν ἄρτον τοῦτον cf. τὸν ἄρτον ἡμῶν τον ἐπιούσιον δὸς ἡμῖν σήμερον in Matthew's version of the Prayer]. . . . And this is the will of my Father, that everyone that beholdeth the Son, and believeth on him, should have eternal life: and I will raise him up at the last day."

19 As especially in the images in Revelation.

20 Cf. on this, and on glory as an expression of the proper satisfaction of desire, C. S. Lewis, "The Weight of Glory" (Transposition and Other Addresses, 1949, pp. 21ff).

21 K. E. Kirk (The Vision of God, 1931, pp. 62f) observes that the prevalent world-accepting outlook of the Jews ensured a high estimate of earthly things, and that "Paradise must be furnished with all that makes for bodily well-being . . . the profusion of the Messianic kingdom will be such that everyone can have his fill of

good things without labour or organisation. Super-terrestrial the joys of Paradise may be, non-terrestrial they are not."

CHAPTER 5

1 Luke's "everyone who . . .", like his "day by day" in the petition for bread, generalizes the petition for continual use.

2 Lohmeyer, op. cit., p. 113.

3 See V. Taylor, *Forgiveness and Reconciliation* (1941), ch. 1, for an examination of the verbs for forgiveness in New Testament.

4 See H. A. Hodges, *The Pattern of Atonement* (1955), for a penetrating study of these.

5 V. Taylor, op. cit., pp. 3ff.

6 It is part of the argument of Anselm's treatise on the Atonement, *Cur Deus Homo?* that man has nothing with which to pay his debts to God in the sense of his sins, since he already owes everything he is and has to God anyway.

7 Charles Williams, *He Came Down from Heaven* and *The Forgiveness of Sins* (1950), p. 160.

8 *De Or.*, 8 (Evans's translation).

9 *De Oratione Dominica*, 25. "This too the Lord of necessity reminds us that we say in prayer: 'And do not let us be brought into temptation'."

10 *De Sermone Domini*, 2, ch. 9. "The sixth petition is 'And bring us not into temptation'. Some manuscripts have the word 'lead', which is, I judge, equivalent in meaning: for both translations have arisen from the one Greek word which is used. But many parties in prayer express themselves thus, 'Suffer us not to be led into temptation'; that is to say, explaining in what sense the word 'lead' is used. For God does not himself lead, but suffers that man be led into temptation whom he has deprived of his assistance, in accordance with a most hidden arrangement, and with his deserts." (Translation in *The Nicene and Post-Nicene Fathers*, vol. 6.)

11 F. P. Harton, *Elements of the Spiritual Life* (1933), ch. 9. Cf. Methodius, *Symposium*, xi, 3: "Eub.—Tell me, do you call anyone a good pilot? Greg.—I certainly do. Eub.—Is it he that saves his

vessel in great and perplexing storms, or is it he who does so in a breathless calm? Greg.—He that does so in a great and perplexing storm. Eub.—Shall we not say then that the soul, which is deluged with the surging waves of the passions, and yet does not, on that account, weary or grow faint, but direct her vessel—that is, the flesh—nobly into the port of chastity, is better and more estimable than he that navigates in calm weather? Greg.—We will say so." (Translation in *Ante-Nicene Fathers*, vol. 14.)

[12] See S. R. Driver on Deut. 6.16. (International Critical Commentary, 1896).

[13] See Charles Williams, op. cit., ch. 2.

[14] See J. A. T. Robinson, *Theology*, February 1947, pp. 43ff.

[15] Mark 14.38,34ff; 13.32f; 14.41. See R. H. Lightfoot, *The Gospel Message of St Mark* (1949), ch. 4.

[16] See *On a Fresh Revision of the New Testament*, 3rd ed. 1891, appendix ii.

[17] The evidence of the New Testament and the Fathers is reviewed by Chase, op. cit., pp. 71ff.

[18] E.g. with Matt. 13.19,38, and probably with Matt. 5.37, but not necessarily with Matt. 5.39. Cf. John 17.15.

[19] This is the question raised by the debate over "demythologizing" the Gospel. See *Kerygma and Myth* (ed. H. W. Bartsch, translated by R. H. Fuller, vol. 1, 1953, vol. 2, 1962), and Hodgson, op. cit., vol. 2, p. 89, who proposes the formula: "What must the truth be, and have been, if it appeared like that to men who thought and wrote as they did?" as a means of decoding biblical statements.

[20] See the analysis of temptation in relation to the spiritual stature of man by R. Niebuhr, *The Nature and Destiny of Man*, (1941), vol. 1, pp. 193ff.

[21] See the discussion of these issues in A. Farrer, *Love Almighty and Ills Unlimited* (1962), ch. 7.

CHAPTER 6

[1] *The Life of Christ in Recent Research* (1907), p. 121.

[2] By A. Loisy, *Le Quatrième Évangile* (2nd ed. 1921), p. 451. This is not incompatible with the view which sees the prayer primarily as

a "Consecration Prayer", perhaps modelled on the Eucharistic Prayer uttered in the early days with a considerable measure of freedom by the celebrant. Cf. E. C. Hoskyns, *The Fourth Gospel* (1940), vol. 2, pp. 585ff.

3 C. K. Barrett, *The Gospel according to St John* (1955), p. 417.

4 John 14.9. Cf. Tertullian (*De Or.* 3): "For we know that the Son is the Father's new name"; (*Adv. Prax.* 23): "*Father, glorify thy name*, in which was the Son."

5 Tertullian (*Adv. Marc.* 4.33) has "In evangelio est dei regnum Christus ipse" ("In the gospel the kingdom of God is Christ himself"). Cyprian (*De Dom. Or.* 13): "But Christ himself too, dearly beloved brethren, can be the kingdom of God, whom every day we desire to come, whose arrival we long to be quickly made manifest to us. For since He Himself is the resurrection, because we rise in Him, so can He also be Himself regarded as the kingdom of God, because we shall reign in Him" (Gee's translation). Origen in his Commentary on Matthew's Gospel coined of Christ the word αὐτοβασιλέια, meaning that in him was the very essence of kingship.

Additional Note

With reference to the discussion of Abba (p. 94 n. 10), it should now be mentioned (1) that J. Jeremias later had doubts about, and withdrew, his suggestion that Abba represented the language of a little child—see his *The Prayers of Jesus,* London 1967, p. 62 and *New Testament Theology,* Vol. 1, *The Proclamation of Jesus,* London 1971, 62ff.; and James Barr, 'Abba Isn't Daddy', *Journal of Theological Studies*, New Series, Vol. 59, pp. 28-47; and (2) that Jeremias' claim that as an address to God Abba was exclusive to Jesus, and therefore a primary clue to his mind, was disputed by G. Vermes, *Jesus the Jew*, London 1973, pp. 210f., and as good as demolished by James Barr, '"Abba Father" and the Familiarity of Jesus', *Theology,* Vol. XCI, 1988, pp. 173-9.

Bibliography

J. L. Houlden, 'Lord's Prayer', in *The Anchor Bible Dictionary*, London 1992, Vol. 4, pp. 356–62 (with bibliography)

E. Lohmeyer, *The Lord's Prayer*, London 1968 (English translation of the work referred to in n. 11, p. 91)

O. Cullman, *Prayer in the New Testament*, London 1995, 37–62

M. J. Goulder, 'The Composition of the Lord's Prayer', *Journal of Theological Studies*, new series, Vol. XIV, 1963, pp. 32–45

R. E. Brown, 'The Pater Noster as an Eschatological Prayer', *New Testament Essays*, New York ³1982, pp. 217–53